The Growing Marijuana Handbook

How To Easily Grow Marijuana and Cannabis Indoor and Outdoors Including Tips on Horticulture, Growing in Small Places and Medical Marijuana - For Beginners and Advanced Growers.

John Lampkin

All Copyrights Reserved

Table Of Contents

Introduction 1

Chapter One : Marijuana And Cannabis: History And Basic Knowledge.. 3

Chapter Two : Seeds: What To Know 9

Chapter 3 : Cultivating The Marijuana Plant.................. 14

Chapter Four : Indoor Growing: Setting Up The Indoor Garden 22

Chapter 5 : Indoor Growing: Planting And Planting Techniques 29

Chapter 6 : Indoor Growing. Nutrients And Environmental Factors.. 41

Chapter 7 : Indoor Growing: Flowering And Breeding ... 50

Chapter Eight : Indoor Growing: Maintaining The Marijuana Plant 59

Chapter Nine : Outdoor Growing: Where And How?..... 64

Chapter Ten : Outdoor Growing: Planting And Planting Techniques 71

Chapter Eleven : Outdoor Growing: Care Of The Growing Plants 78

Chapter Twelve : Outdoor Growing: Nutrients And Environmental Factors... 86

Chapter Thirteen : Outdoor Growing: Flowering And Breeding 92

Chapters Fourteen : Harvesting The Marijuana Plants .. 99

Chapter Fifteen : After Harvesting, What's Next?! 105

Conclusion 109

Introduction

Today, the name "Cannabis" rings a bell in the minds of every teenager in the world. This is clearly not for its medicinal usage or benefit, but for the reputation of its abuse and irresponsible usage by those who want to "get high". This notion has tainted the cannabis plant to be a deadly poison one must abstain from.

However, this is not true. Cannabis has, in fact, become more of a help than hindrance to man. This concept and more are what this handbook will delve into as it enlightens you even further. Growing cannabis could prove to be a big endeavor at first, but with the help of this handbook, you will easily scale through the steps.

From the beginning to the end, this handbook will cover every detail of marijuana growing. You'll become conversant with not just the life cycle of the cannabis plant but also its uses, benefits, and economic importance. Rest assured, at the end of this handbook comes enlightenment, fresh ideas, and an awesome experience. Unless your plan to grow cannabis is not curtailed by several factors which include the law, financial capability, and time, this handbook will equip you with all the knowledge you need to be an effective grower.

Have you been experiencing bad growth with your cannabis plants? Then this handbook is just perfect for you. It will pinpoint the mistakes you've made so you can correct them next time. It's going to be a bumper harvest - year in, year out. Read through the chapters from beginning to the end, so as to get an idea of what the book is talking about.

In the end, we greatly hope that this handbook will help you achieve your goal of not only growing cannabis, but also growing a healthy-looking cannabis plant.

Sit tight, have fun, and enjoy the ride!

Chapter One
Marijuana and Cannabis: History and Basic Knowledge

Historically, cannabis, which is also known as marijuana, weed, and dope, has existed since the beginning of mankind. It has served as a help to man for both medical and recreational purposes. As a psychoactive herb, the cannabis plant blossoms in an environment which is not devoid of adequate water, sunlight, and temperature.

As one hell of a stubborn plant, cannabis can sprout out of any environment whatsoever – valley, plain, hill or even edgy lands. History has it that the cannabis seeds were mostly planted accidentally around the world either by the winds, birds in the sky, or attached to the hoofs of animals traveling on foot. Little wonder why the cannabis plant is very adaptive to both indoor and outdoor conditions.

Notwithstanding, the historical background and origin of the cannabis plant can be debatable, as there is no consensus on how its life began. Since, it has gained popularity with special improvements, modifications, and upgrades to aid its growth.

When the name "Cannabis" or "Marijuana" pops up, an average individual with little or no knowledge about the plant would most definitely think about the abuse and illegal use of the - which to a large extent has tainted the good name of the cannabis plant. However, there is more to it. The cannabis plant can serve many benefits.

To begin with, cannabis dates back to the era of our ancestors. They used the cannabis plant for quite a number of things. The early 1900s showcased a time when the cannabis plant was vehemently used in the textile industry to create fabrics as a result of its strong nature and ability to withstand a large amount of stress.

This was known as "Hemp" and was proven to be a far better option than the ordinary cotton used today. In reality, what this means is that people had to own minimal clothing items as they could stand the test of time. And guess what? It didn't go down well with the fabric industry. Owning few items means low patronage, and low patronage means low profit.

Now guess what they did next? Your guess is as good as mine! Propaganda and stereotypes were churned up about the cannabis plant during that period. And, yes - they succeeded. The government restricted cannabis to a very large extent. Ever since then, there have been a great number of crusades and campaigns against the cannabis plant.

The stereotypes that go along with the cannabis plant have tainted the real usefulness of the plant, thereby clouding the minds of everyone with propaganda and false ideas. Here are some of the accusations levied on the cannabis plant:

1. Cannabis is abused and harmful.
2. Cannabis is addictive.
3. People die from the intake of cannabis.
4. Cannabis addiction cannot be easily curbed.

These notions are not entirely true. Yes, the cannabis plant is being abused as its leaves are sold as dope, weed, or greens by hoodlums and miscreants. But make no mistake, the decision to abuse the effects of the cannabis plant lies entirely with the abuser.

As a psychoactive herb or plant, the cannabis plant can be very much addictive. According to propaganda, the plant, leaves, and seeds contain the THC, or the tetrahydrocannabinol, which makes the cannabis addictive and hard to rehabilitate. This is not true. Although, THC, or the tetrahydrocannabinol chemical, in the cannabis plant goes a long way in creating hallucinations, delusions, and change of thinking, its addiction lies solely with the abuser.

As a matter of fact, there has been no record of anyone that has died from the intake of cannabis. This notion is simply exaggerated. It is so obvious that death scares would work magic as people tend to stay clear of such activities. Law enforcement agencies have been created, promotions and campaigns embarked on, and laws formulated – thereby hiding the real objective behind these flimsy excuses.

It is important to note that cannabis addiction can be curbed via psychotherapy.

Therefore, when people hear the word "cannabis", what comes to mind is the normal greens, weed, skunk, or dope wrapped in a dirty sheet of paper sold on the street. Far from this, there are lots of advantages and benefits attached to the use of the cannabis plant. This handbook promises to enlighten and hopefully change your perception of the cannabis plant.

Importance of the Cannabis Plant

The importance of the cannabis plant to man can be classified into different segments – Health benefits and Economic benefits.

• Health Benefits:

To begin with, research has shown that the cannabis plant has more than 20 health benefits to mankind as a whole. A study on cannabis embarked on by the National Eye Institute in the 1970s shows that the plant can be used to cure Glaucoma (a severe eye defect). It slows down the rapid growth of the disease and, as a result, prevents blindness.

Cannabis also helps to control seizures that occur in people suffering from Epilepsy. This was tested and proven in a study in 2003 by Robert J. Delorenzo and has proven to be effective ever since.

Cannabis also goes a long way in improving the condition of the lungs - unlike its counterpart, tobacco, which damages them. The Journal of the American Medical Association laid emphasis on this.

More than ever today, cannabis intake has proven to be effective in the fight against cancer. The California Pacific Medical Center showcased this in their reports, pointing out how cannabis can stop the spread of cancer further in the host body. What cannabis does is to mute the Id-1 gene, thereby replicating the gene into millions of replicas to fight the cancer by spreading through the host body. This way, cancer is curtailed to an extent.

Have you ever wondered why cannabis users are mostly slim and fit? Well, cannabis intake helps a lot in burning down fat in the body. Not only that - it also helps you achieve a much healthier metabolism.

- **Economic Benefits:**

To a very large extent, cannabis would have a positive impact on the revenue of a government, firm, or even individuals. The sale of this plant, its roots, or its leaves could generate more than enough income, which in turn could raise the standard of living in the region.

Mass growth of the cannabis plant would create what is calculated to be millions of new jobs. Are you wondering where the jobs would come from? It's pretty simple. Jobs like cannabis growers, processors, distributors, retailers, inspectors, and much more along the cannabis line would be available for people to engage themselves in - and in turn, make a living from.

Species

There are basically three types of Cannabis species.

1. **Sativa:** Sativas are tall, lengthy cannabis plants with pointed ends on their leaves. The leaves are also free from any marks or patterns. There is a presence of long internodes which exist in between branches from 3 inches to 6 inches.

2. **Indica:** Indicas are quite short, unlike their tall sativa counterparts. They are the direct opposite of sativa as they possess short internodes and bear marble-like patterns in their round shaped leaves.

3. **Ruderalis:** Ruderalis are also short cannabis plants of about 6 inches long. Their leaves are small and thick. Their internodes are also short with lots of branching space in between.

Cannabis has been in existence for a very long time. Our ancestors used it, mastered it, and applied it effectively in curbing and curing many diseases, defects, and deficiencies. This chapter is geared toward showing you the light as regards cannabis and helping you see the plant from a whole new point of view.

Legalizing the growing of cannabis would open a new path that will lead to development, change, and prosperity unlike the lies, propaganda, and stereotypes churned up to defame the plant.

Chapter Two
Seeds: What to Know

Like all plants, the cannabis plant begins with the seed. Presently, the cannabis plant seeds range to over 400 varieties and each seed is quite potent. However, some supersede others in terms of potency, growth, and the ability to thrive under harsh weather condition.

As a grower, you can either plant the seeds individually or a crossbreed of more than one species. But the question remains - how can you differentiate which seeds are the best? It's pretty simple. Along the course of this chapter, we will explain what you should look out for while selecting seeds.

Getting a seed with high quality is paramount. Having a conducive environment with adequate water, temperature, and sunlight contributes to a better harvest. But, getting good quality seeds is of great importance. You can either go for plain/pure seeds or the much-preferred crossbreed seeds.

The plain seeds are generally available in the market while the crossbreeds are limited because of the planting experiments they are used for by breeders. The classification of the seeds are as follows:

1. **Pure Sativa:** These are plain and pure species without no mixtures whatsoever.

2. **Sativa:** This species comprises of generally the mixture of Sativa and Indica.

3. **Pure Indica:** These are plain and pure species without no mixtures whatsoever.

4. **Indica:** This species comprises of generally the mixture of Indica and Sativa

5. **Indica/Sativa:** This is the equal combination of both Sativa and Indica species.

6. **Ruderalis:** These are species that are plain and pure.

Therefore, when you are in the market to purchase cannabis seeds, be sure to check the classification, features, and ratios of the crossbreeds so as to get the best quality. There are occasions where the combination of the crossbreeds might not be equal, thus making it's plants lean towards one side of the ratio more than the other.

Having an in-depth knowledge of this would give you an idea of what to expect as your crossbreed seeds start germinating. Notwithstanding, the grower can also exert an influence in keeping the growth, length, and look of the cannabis plant exactly how he or she wants it to be. The style, time, and technique we employ in harvesting our cannabis plant also play a part in influencing the high type.

Harvesting it later after it is ripe induces a couch-lock effect. On the other hand, harvesting the cannabis plant beforehand only leads to a cerebral high.

Choosing the Seeds

With over 400 varieties of seeds to choose from, getting the right seeds for your garden shouldn't be hard to pull off. However, knowing which cannabis seed is perfect for indoor and outdoor is paramount. In this case, we would recommend you stick to the breeder's instructions or advice.

To this effect, indoor cannabis seeds should be planted strictly indoors while the outdoor cannabis seeds should also be planted outside for much better results. Nevertheless, you might want to be a little more adventurous - and there is room for that. You can decide to interchange the seeds and substitute the indoor seeds for outdoor seeds and vice versa. The end result might even be much more productive in the long run.

After a careful selection of both indoor and outdoor seeds, the next best thing to do is to check the flowering times. Flowering times in the cannabis plant differ from one species to another. Naturally, flowering in the cannabis plant comes after the germination and vegetative growth of the plant.

Thus, endeavor to check the seed bank's instructions and manuals so as to stay abreast of all the necessary information about the seed you will eventually choose. For example, the seed bank might state that the period of 7-9 weeks after germination is the flowering time of the cannabis plant. This would give you an idea of when to start preparing for harvest.

The appearance and feel of the seeds are also paramount when choosing a seed. Seeds that look fresh, and healthy are always of good quality. However, with some seeds it is hard to tell from their appearance alone. Seeds of great quality exhibit coloring that is far darker on the outside.

Sometimes, they come in grey colors with a touch of tiger stripes. They are often firm and can stand the test of time. They are also hard as weak seeds end up cracking when pressure is applied to it.

Types of Cannabis Seeds

1. **Feminized Seeds:** This type of Cannabis seed is the most populous you would find around. According to research, 95% of the germinated feminized seeds end up yielding feminine cannabis plants. To this effect, there are lots of benefits associated with the feminized seeds. They produce buds, which makes pollination unnecessary. With more than enough space, adequate sunlight, and good temperature, the feminized seeds are bound to grow well and offer a bountiful harvest. The three best examples of the feminized seeds are Amnesia Haze, Afghan Skunk, and Yellow Lemon Haze.

2. **Autoflowering Seeds:** As a unique and improved cannabis seed, autoflowering seeds have the strength and ability to thrive even in severe weather conditions. The autoflowering seeds grow within the

period of 10 weeks before the plant automatically blossoms with flowers, which indicates the beginning of its peak. They are a mixture of both male and female. Autoflowering plants are quite shorter than those from feminized seeds. The three best examples of autoflowering seeds are AK 47 AUTO, Amnesia Haze AUTO, and the Low Rider AUTO.

3. **Regular Cannabis Seeds:** These seeds germinate into male and female cannabis plants. Often times, they are equal in numbers, especially during harvest. Regular cannabis seeds were the first of the cannabis seeds; that was long before the Feminized and Autoflowering seeds came into being. As a traditional type of seed, they require more care and attention poured into them for a proper turn out.

Don't get it twisted, all cannabis plants need special care and attention poured toward them for a proper and perfect bloom. However, some seeds just demand it more than the rest. With over 400 seeds at your fingertips, choose wisely. Endeavor to weigh all possible outcomes and options before choosing a seed for your dope garden.

Don't be afraid to try a new mix of crossbreeds. It all depends on the kind of weed you want to grow. You can even try out personal seeds sourced from a friend's cannabis garden. The outcome might be mind-blowing. But the most important thing still remains, a good quality seed begets a strong and healthy plant. Now, let's move to the next chapter, shall we?

Chapter 3
Cultivating the Marijuana Plant

By now, I am sure you must be familiar with what cannabis entails and the kinds of seed you would like to use for your garden. As a grower who wants to start cultivating the marijuana plant, either as a beginner or a professional, you have to consider some stumbling factors as well as ask yourself important questions beyond venturing into it.

Cultivating marijuana is not child's play, especially with a large number of campaigns and crusades programmed against it. The government, to a large extent, has been able to restrict the growth and distribution of cannabis by arresting and prosecuting growers and distributors. The system seems to kick against it. Thus, cultivating a garden of weed takes courage, tact, and carefulness.

Hitherto, there is no actual offense to being caught with seeds, leaves, or any other parts of the cannabis plant. However, cultivating the plant is an unlawful act which is punishable by the law. What makes the sale of the plant punishable is the "trafficking offense" tag labeled on it - and it comes with no less than 10 years imprisonment. Cultivating cannabis is a serious offense.

So, before leaping into this business, we would suggest you take a good look as well. Ensure no stones are left unturned. Ask yourself these compelling questions:

1. Are you going to be around always to look after your garden of weed? If not, do you have someone trustworthy for that job?
2. How good is the security of the site?
3. Is it spacious enough to hide the smell?
4. How secure is your grow room?

These and more are important questions you should ask yourself before starting cultivation. Growing marijuana can be a lot easier than you might imagine. If all your answers to these questions are yes, then we would say you are one step away from being an expert grower. Be that as it may, a lot of people have been growing cannabis peacefully both indoors and outdoors without attracting a third party. Now, the question you should ask yourself is – are you ready to be a part of those smart men?

One rule all growers of the cannabis plant abide by is "Never Tell Anyone That You Are Growing Cannabis." This is the most sacred rule of them all; the same rule that has guided the privileged "Smart Men" to continuous, stress-free cultivation of the cannabis plant all through harvest periods. Additionally, in this line of business, you cannot afford to have loose lips around you. Like the saying goes, loose lips sink ships.

Let's take Simon, for example:

Simon is a fun loving person with a deep passion for cannabis. Once in a while, he smoked it along with his friends during parties or home picnics. He wanted to start growing his own weed instead of getting it from the street, but he had no idea how to even begin. Then Boom! He came across the "Growing Marijuana Handbook." He had since become an expert grower in his own home.

Don't get it twisted, Simon shares his weed - but with a cover-story. "Hey, Guys! Look what I just bought downtown?" "A friend just gave me greens as a gift for a job well done. Let's share." These stories and more have saved Simon's life and garden a million times. My point is: **Be. Like. Simon.** Some of your friends might not be good at keeping secrets. Keeping your garden away from the public is what will help you become a better and expert grower.

Cultivating cannabis is a serious business that must be handled with passion and enthusiasm. You must be willing to treat your garden like it's a part of you. That is the only way you will give it the necessary care and attention it needs to thrive. Regardless of the kind of species you are growing, the kind of special seeds you are sowing, and the kind of improved cannabis plant you want to cultivate, if you don't take good care of the plant, it will eventually die off.

Cannabis Life Cycle

Cannabis is unique. It is special. Unlike most plants that feature a 6 stage life cycle, the cannabis plant has just 3 main stages. Want to know them? Here they are:

1. Germination:

Germination is the first stage toward the cultivation of cannabis either in a large, medium, or small scale production. You can't just assume getting the seeds is enough. No wind, birds, or animals are going to fly or walk through your garden and accidentally start sowing your seeds for you. And trust me, sowing can be quite fun.

Putting a seed or two in the soil is always the first thing to do. With much care and proper gardening, the seeds crack open, bringing forth a newborn seedling on the surface of the soil. Its root begins to spread like tentacles, catching a firm hold of the soil beneath. This gives balance to the seedling whilst it shoots up.

When sunlight touches this young seedling, it paves the way for fresh leaves, thereby pushing the seed's shell far away from itself. This is the beginning of life for a cannabis plant. Whether it will grow into full maturity from here now solely depends on the type of care, attention, and techniques you employ afterwards. Naturally, this germination process takes place in the span of three weeks.

Now guess what happens afterwards? Tons of fresh leaves end up sprouting with quite a number of marijuana characteristics. The leaves start forming finger shapes, the edges start getting pointy, and the stems start getting thicker. This is known as the seedling stage. I would advise you use a stick or a wooden stake to hold the seedlings in an upright position. Replace the sticks if you have to, because this phase lasts three good weeks, setting the pace for the plant to sail through to the second stage – Vegetative Growth.

2. Vegetative Growth:

The vegetative growth of any cannabis plant irrespective of the species is usually the same. Little by little, the seedling begins to gain energy from the adequate sunlight, temperature, and water it comes in contact with. With time, the leaves begin to get bigger and the stem becomes thicker. Telling the sex of the plant would be quite glaring at this stage of the cycle.

Most times, the vegetative growth stage also marks the beginning of the pre-flowering period. Ensure you are well-prepared as your marijuana plant hits the road to maturity.

The pre-flowering phase paves way for the flowering stage. One distinctive feature during this phase is the slowed-down growth of the plant. This stage triggers a new development which focuses on filling out, instead of growing tall. Also, calyx will appear at strategic points. With this change, the stems are bound to grow thicker, leaves wider and fuller, and the branches sprout out even more.

Clip off unwanted parts. By now, your plant must be able to stand upright without sticks or stakes. No doubt, the vegetative growth stage is the pathway toward our next stage of the cycle – the Flowering Stage.

3. Flowering Stage:

The flowering stage comes right before the harvest period. You might want to hold on tight to something as you behold the beauty and sight of the blooming flowers of the cannabis plant. The flowering stage showcases full-fledged, beautiful flowers that will surely blow your mind away.

The sex of each plant becomes more glaringly obvious at this stage. The male plant will showcase a collection of grape-like balls while the female plant will feature whitish pistils around its leaves. However, flowers in the cannabis plant take time to fully develop.

To this effect, something amazing will happen as the plant keeps pushing towards maturity. The male plants' pollen sacks will reach a point where they will burst, thereby dispersing the pollen to the female flowers. In turn, the female plant will reciprocate by making seeds out of that pollen. The seeds stay in the female buds for weeks before they attain maturity.

You might be surprised as a beginner when your plants start dripping liquid. No need to worry, as your plant is approaching maturity. Those liquids are called resins. Resins are formed as a result of the large size of the buds which would make your plant very sticky when you touch them.

The cannabis plant growth system can be likened to the normal system of an animal in heat. Wondering if that makes sense? Then here is my comparison. Animals in heat showcase their need for an opposite-sex partner, in order to copulate amongst themselves. Failure to meet with one leads to not-so-good reactions like aggressiveness, stress, and abnormal behaviors from the animal.

This is the same way the female cannabis plant reacts to the absence of pollen from a male plant. Instead of being aggressive, stressed, and abnormal, it produces resins from the big, swollen buds, which are trying hard to attract the male pollen. This signals the beginning of harvest and full maturity of the cannabis plant.

How do you know they are mature? It's pretty simple! The white female pistils change colors, thereby opening the seedpods automatically. During this phase, it is advisable that you stay alert, so you can collect the seeds yourself before they end up being dispersed on the floor.

Cultivating cannabis means tending to the plants, watering them at the necessary time, weeding out an unwanted plant that may hinder its growth, and so much more. It's a total devotion that must be adhered to.

There you have it! Cultivating cannabis at your fingertips! Like you were promised at the beginning of this Handbook, by the time you finish reading through it, you will be more enlightened about the cannabis plant than when you first picked it up. Don't forget to space your cannabis plants. That way, they won't be competing for adequate air, water, and sunlight, which might, in turn, lead to unbalanced growth in your weed.

Cannabis cultivation varies in techniques. The indoor growing style is quite different from outdoor. This and more are what we will explain in the next chapters. Discover how to properly start up an indoor dope garden. You wouldn't want to miss it. And remember, always be like Simon - courageous, tactful, and very careful.

Chapter Four
Indoor Growing: Setting Up the Indoor Garden

Having learned about the basic concepts, history, seedlings, and steps of cultivating cannabis in the previous chapters, the next thing to focus on is one of the core production stages, which is transferring your seedlings to the permanent growing area. This area or environment will be the home for your seedlings for the next 3 to 6 months.

In Chapter Three, we asked vital questions as regards growing cannabis. If answered correctly, this would ease the stumbling block between you and the success of your dope garden. Choosing a conducive, quiet, nice place for your garden can be quite hard to pull off. However, there are necessary factors you would have to consider before choosing a great site.

Before then, a decision needs to be made! Are you planning on cultivating your cannabis plants indoor, or growing them outdoor? Ask yourself this question. If your answer is the former, then we would suggest you read this chapter with rapt attention. Indoor cannabis gardens started decades ago with the heavy price placed on the necks of cannabis cultivators. Growers of cannabis had to crawl back into their shells, if their lives and businesses meant anything to them.

Crawling back means only one thing. Re-strategizing and re-planning. Thus, indoor cannabis cultivation was born. Law enforcement agencies could no longer smell their presence even from afar. Indoor growing became the only way to keep growers' heads up sitting on their necks.

Cannabis growers no longer had any other option other than to focus, experiment, and perfect indoor gardening. Indoor gardening, to a large extent, helped lots of growers carry on with their activities with little or no worries from the authorities. Indoor growing gives them the perfect cover they crave.

Additionally, indoor growing simply means what the term implies; growing a plant or crop indoors. This can be either at home, at a business area, or in an enclosed environment. This method of farming involves the use of hydroponics and artificial or natural lightning to provide the essential nutrients needed by the plant. Cannabis cultivation thrives under this indoor method of growing cannabis.

Setting Up the Indoor Garden

Now, setting up the permanent area or environment to grow your product is essential. No doubt, there are lots of factors to consider, issues to tackle, and problems to address. Amongst these important factors lies privacy and security. In order words, privacy and security, to a large extent, play a very big part in choosing the site.

How secure is the environment? Is it a secluded area? How many people know about the site? Can it withhold the smell when it blossoms? How secure is it when people visit you? These and more are questions you should ask yourself before setting up an indoor dope garden of your own.

Like we said earlier, the factors to consider are quite numerous. In order to set up a state-of-the-art indoor garden, no matter how low your budget is, tackling these factors that would end up causing obstacles to your precious plants is of great importance. This will help prevent failure in your quest to grow good and healthy cannabis indoors.

There are many factors, like your financial capability, the right lighting to use in order to avoid overcooking the cannabis, the right place to show your cannabis seeds with enough privacy and security, etc. The factors are numerous, thus discussing each and every one of them would be impossible. Therefore, we would pick just a few. Follow us, as we will be discussing more details on these factors below:

1. Lighting

Lighting is the most important factor to consider when growing cannabis indoors, and there are two major ways to generate light for your products. These are natural lighting and artificial lighting. These two ways, even when perfect for an indoor garden, come with their strengths and flaws. For instance, if you are looking to produce bigger flowers (more buds), then artificial indoor lighting is the best. But if you are looking to spend less, natural window lighting is perfect for you.

Still not following? Then let's break it down for you. Artificial lighting yields more product but it's very expensive to run. While its counterpart, natural lighting, is relatively cheap, it offers fewer yields. Thus, if you are trying to run the artificial lighting method of growing cannabis indoors, then it is very important for you to consider your electricity bills and the kind of light to use.

Hence, you have to think of how much electrical power will be consumed. How much heat will be generated from the lamps? And how much light will be emitted from the lamps? Modern-day cannabis growers tend to use three major artificial light sources that are very effective. These are:

1. High-Intensity Discharge Lamps (HID).
2. Compact Fluorescent Light (CFL)
3. Light Emitting Diode (LED).

These lights can be used separately or in combination, but you have to be careful how you combine the lights so as not to overcook your cannabis.

On the other hand, if you are looking to run much cheaper cultivation of cannabis, which equates to using the natural window lighting method of growing, then taking into consideration the privacy and security of your cultivation are of great importance. Light to the cannabis plant is one important nutrient it needs to thrive. And the natural lighting method of indoor cultivating can only be accessed via sunlight, or window light.

To this effect, it is important to place the cannabis plant in a strategic position near a window where light can easily reach and penetrate the plant. To get the strategic position you need, you have to note that the sun rises in the east and sets in the west, just as it travels north or south depending on your location. As a result of this, you have to study the sun's position in your location in order to achieve a desirable result.

Before you do that, though, you have to make sure your cultivation is safe by considering whether people can look up and see cannabis by the window or if people who wash your windows can easily spot the cannabis through them Also, note that the sativa plants usually grow very big and can be easily spotted. So it is important you take these factors into consideration before delving into the natural window light method of growing cannabis.

2. Growing Space

Another factor to consider when running an indoor method of growing cannabis is your growing space. This could be a whole room or part of a room dedicated to the cultivation. Places like the basement, attic, spare bathroom, hot press, and closet are good locations to start cannabis cultivation. You can even decide to build your own cabinet specifically for the cultivation. Also, note that some of these locations need artificial light to enhance growth.

3. Time

Timing is an essential factor when it comes to indoor cannabis growing, especially when you are running a natural window lighting cultivation. This helps you determine and plan toward the season when the sun is at its peak. For instance, if the sun is at its peak in the month of July, then it is advisable you start producing seedlings as early as late March, April, and May.

Therefore, it is essential and very important for a cannabis grower, in general, to be able to predict and guess when they will get the best weather. This factor helps the grower foresee the harvest time for their cannabis cultivation, especially when they coordinate this with the flower times as instructed by the breeder.

4. Soil

The soil is another factor to consider when setting up indoor cannabis growing. For the fact that you can't cultivate cannabis outside on a plantation or farm because of security and privacy, and buying the expensive Hydroponic Substrates is also not an option, finding the right soil for cultivation is the next best thing to do when setting up your indoor growing. As a matter of fact, it doesn't cost a cent.

Nevertheless, you just can't jump at any soil you see in your environment. Fertile or not, not all soils work hand-in-hand with cannabis. Like we said in our previous chapters, cannabis is special and it is unique. Thus, here are the three things to consider when choosing a good soil in order to grow healthy plants:

1. pH
2. Structure
3. Nutrients

Also note that the use of soil in growing gives your cannabis a certain taste and aroma.

Setting up an indoor cannabis garden is very easy if you are willing to take the chance. With determination, planning, and dedication, your weed garden will be up and running in no time. Just ensure all boxes are checked, no stones are left unturned, and all measures are taken for a perfect cannabis cultivation indoors. Join us in the next chapters where more of these factors will be followed up and discussed in clearer details.

Chapter 5
Indoor Growing: Planting and Planting Techniques

Indoor growing of cannabis is very easy to practice when you have the right set-up and I am certain you already have an idea of what your indoor garden should be like from the previous chapter. In this chapter, we will be focused on planting properly and the planting techniques you can use to achieve a masterpiece indoor garden.

There are so many ways to grow cannabis indoors, and selecting which to practice is totally dependent on what you can afford and what is best for you. Moving forward in this chapter, we will be focusing on the two major methods or ways of growing cannabis indoors. These ways are Soil Growing and Hydroponics.

Soil Growing

Soil growing is one of the easiest and least expensive methods of growing marijuana indoors. With the right soil growing set-up, you are sure to cultivate and harvest a delicious and amazing crop of cannabis. With an effective light system already in place, the next thing to focus on is the right soil combination for your soil growing set-up.

Choosing the Right Soil for Indoor Soil Growing

Choosing the right soil for your indoor growing is very important as there are many types and varieties of soil out there to choose from. But this shouldn't be a problem, because as we proceed, you will find out that different ingredients can be added to different soils to achieve a healthy and improved cannabis plant growth.

When growing cannabis, the soil you use goes through different phases and periods. In the first period or phase, the soil contains water and other nutrients which the cannabis' long, winding roots absorb in order to grow. During the other period or phase, the soil becomes dry, and this could be as a result of the absorbing of most of the soil water by the cannabis plant root or as a result of you not watering your plant.

Do not panic, because in these dry periods, air finds its way into the soil and allows the roots of your cannabis plant to breathe. As we mentioned in the previous chapter, there are three major factors to look out for when choosing a soil for cannabis indoor growing. These are the pH, soil structure, and nutrients. Here's why these factors are important and essential for your indoor growing soil.

Factors to Look Out For

1. **PH:** Soil pH helps you determine the acidity and the alkalinity of a soil. A soil pH is measured on a scale from 0 to 14, where 0 is very acidic, 7 is neutral, and 14 is very alkaline. The pH of soil is usually written on the bag. Now, for growing a cannabis plant, you

need a soil that is neutral because if it is above or below 7, it can cause problems to the growth of your cannabis plant.

Therefore, go to any gardening shop and get a small pH meter so you can measure the overall pH of the soil you are going to be using for your indoor soil growing.

2. **Nutrients:** There are three basic nutrients found in soil. These are: Nitrogen, Phosphorus, and Potassium, popularly known as NPK. The percentage ratio for NPK is usually 20:20:20. In other words, 20% Nitrogen, 20% Phosphorus and 20% Potassium. The remaining 40% represents other particles that make up the soil, including liquid, which is usually water.

This information can be found on the bag of the soil you are buying. It is also important to note that these ratios can change because of different types of soil brand and nutrients, so it is essential to know the right percentages of the different nutrients your cannabis plants need. Based on research, we have come to understand that cannabis plants require a higher level of Nitrogen, and normal levels of Phosphorus and Potassium during vegetative growth.

Therefore, when picking out a soil, you need to pick a bag that contains all three nutrients. This is also applicable when picking out chemical fertilizers. Look for a mixture with the highest first number or a first number that is equal to the other numbers. In other words, the ratio of 12:12:12

or 20:20:20 is fine and the best you can find out there. 12:6:6 and 18:4:5 are also fine and work great for your indoor grow.

A ratio like 8:20:20, on the other hand, is not suitable for cannabis plant growth. This is because soil with a higher Phosphorus level is best for flowering plants, not cannabis.

3. **Structure:** The best soil structure to look out for your indoor soil growing is a soil that is not too moist. Hence, pick out a soil that easily dries out and doesn't hold water like a muddy soil, as this can sometimes cause damage to your plant because of the lack of air. The roots of the cannabis need air to breathe.

Also, pick out a soil that is not too dry and will not need to be watered very often. In other words, you need to find a soil that balances the two (wetness and dryness), a soil that is loose but feels fine and kind of heavy when touched.

Choosing a soil is totally up to you so you have to be careful not to pick out a soil that is too soft and weightless or too hard and bulky. Medium soft and heavy is the kind of structure your cannabis plant seeks.

Soil Types Suitable for Growing

At this point, it is important for you to note that you cannot just bring in natural outdoor soil for the cultivation of cannabis because the soil may end up not being sterile and may contain pests and bugs that will affect your plant. It is advisable for an indoor grower to always purchase soil from a garden shop. In this part of the chapter, we are going to be discussing some of the soil types and why they are suitable or not very suitable for planting cannabis.

There are many different types of soil medium out there that marijuana can grow on, but some of these soils may not be very suitable for marijuana cultivation. Below is a list of the different types of soil and their effect on marijuana.

1. **Sand and Silt soils:** Sandy soils are usually pure sands or a mixture of sand and soil. As a result of this, sandy soils are very dry and easily drain out water and other minerals too quickly from the soil. This soil is therefore not suitable for our needs in growing cannabis.

On the other hand, silt soils are like sandy soil but darker and more clay-like. They have the ability to hold other nutrients but cannot hold water like sandy soils. In essence, sandy soils and silt soils are not suitable in our quest to achieve a successful indoor marijuana garden.

2. **Clay Soil:** Clay is a stiff fine-grained type of soil that contains hydrated aluminosilicate which makes the soil flexible when water is added. This type of soil is certainly not very suitable for the growth of marijuana and is rarely used for its cultivation. It is only acceptable to use this when it is mixed with other types of soil.

3. **Humus:** Humus soil constitutes organic matters which are created by the decomposition of plants.

This type of soil is also sometimes known as compost, which is the final mixture of manure from organic matters. Loamy soil and other mediums are added to complete the mixture of this soil. Humus soil can be purchased from any local gardening store.

4. **Loamy Soil:** Loamy soil is a mixture of all the above three types of soil; sand, silt, clay, and humus. This type of soil is very fertile and highly recommended for your indoor growing. The information containing the mixture of the soil is always found on the bag and it is very likely you will find this type of soil in a local shop.

Choosing the Right Pot

Having chosen the perfect soil for cannabis cultivation from a local gardening store, the next thing to look out for is the right pot. Planting pots come in different sizes, shapes, colors, and abilities to add certain benefits to your plants. When choosing the right pot to grow your marijuana in, you need to look out for a much larger pot of about 1.5 to 3-gallons because cannabis tends to develop long roots.

Another thing to look out for when picking the right cannabis planting pot, especially if you are a newbie in indoor cannabis growing, is perforated pots. These are pots that come with holes or perforations at the bottom. These perforated pots sit on a dish which helps retain drained water from the soil after watering. You are expected to change the dish after a while.

The reason for these perforated pots is to control and drain excess water from the soil, especially when the plant is overwatered. Overwatering is very bad for your cannabis plants as it can kill your plant, waste nutrients, and cost you time. In other words, you have to be extra careful not to overwater your plants.

After getting your pot, it is expected for you to clean it properly in order to rid the pot of all unwanted chemicals, particles, or dust it has gathered over time. Also, it is best to use one pot per plant, so if there's a problem with the plant, nutrient, soil, and watering, then it will affect only one plant.

Indoor Soil Growing

There are a lot of options to consider when you want to cultivate cannabis indoors. Below, we are going to list and explain 4 most common indoor setups. These are:

1. Bench growing Technique

Bench growing has to do with growing cannabis on a bench or table which is made of aluminum or wood. The pots where the plants are cultivated will be placed on the bench or table for growing. The bench growing method is mostly used by commercial marijuana producers.

2. SOG (Sea of Green) Growing

SOG growing or Sea Of Green growing is a process of growing cannabis where, at a young age of cultivation, flowering is forced. This method of growing enables you to harvest earlier than the normal harvest time and allows you to maximize space without sacrificing your yields. This method also enables fitting more flowering plants into a small space.

SOG Growing Technique Steps

1. Germinate seeds or create clones.
2. With 18 to 24-hour lights, grow your plants to reach 10 or 12 inches in height.
3. Space your plants and increase lighting regimen to 12/12 in order to force flowering.
4. When you finally achieve a dense canopy, trip branches from bottom to use them for the clone.
5. Harvest!
6. Grow again.

1. ScrOG (Screen of Green) Growing Technique

The ScrOG or Screen of Green growing technique has to do with growing marijuana indoors with the aid of screens to maximize light exposure and horizontal growth. Chicken wire or nylon netting can be used to influence the movement and growth of marijuana on the screen. It is expected that your screen has holes with a diameter of 5cm. This method is mostly used when your grow room has limited space for growing.

ScrOG Growing Technique Steps

1. Place your screen 20 to 25 inches from your plants.
2. Cut the top cola off of each plant.
3. When the top of each plant reaches the screen, prune bottom branches.
4. After two days of pruning the bottom, force plant into flowering.
5. Use chicken wire or nylon netting to attach all branches to the screen horizontally.
6. Start growing!

1. Cabinet Growing Technique

The cabinet growing technique is another easy and efficient way of growing cannabis indoors. If you have limited space or are just trying to experiment as a newbie or beginner, you can start by practicing cabinet growing. This entails growing your cannabis plant in a small space like a closet, cabinet, growth tent, or grow box.

Cabinet Growing Technique Steps

1. Clean and clear a cabinet or closet space properly ridding the space of molds, dust, and dirt.
2. Paint inside the cabinet or closet, with preferably white paint, or use a strong white plastic to cover inside the cabinet.
3. Set up the lights.
4. Put your potted plant in place.

5. Set up fans and carbon filters.
6. Start growing!

Hydroponics

Hydroponics is another efficient and effective way of growing marijuana indoors if you are not looking to use the soil growing method. Hydroponics is the growing of plants in gravel, sand, or liquid, without the presence of soil. Nutrients are added in the process of hydroponics to increase growth.

In other words, when growing marijuana with this method, soil is not going to be used and the medium for plant growth is definitely going to be sterile and inert. Plants grow faster because this method provides your plant with nutrients, air, and water. The hydroponic method of indoor growing is really great to practice and is ideal for areas that are frequently in drought.

From the previous discussions, we have come to understand that marijuana plants require certain nutrients to promote its growth and quality. Without these nutrients, it is very likely that your plants will die. Under the soil growing method, we came to the conclusion that the soil provides the marijuana plants with nutrients like NPK for better growth.

It is also important to know how to add nutrients to your plants when practicing the hydroponic method of growing. This can be done by creating a balanced nutrition solution containing Nitrogen, Phosphorus, Potassium,

Calcium, sulfur, and magnesium mixed with water. This method also makes it easy to adjust nutrient levels for the different stages of growth.

Just like the soil growing methods, there are different hydroponic techniques you could use for your indoor growing. These are:

Ebb and Flow Method

This is the simplest and most common method of hydroponic indoor growing. It is perfect for beginners. This method involves the use of 3 reservoirs, one holding the water and nutrients needed for your growing, the second holding clean tap water that can be reserved for 2 to 3 days, and the third as a spare in case either of the other two breaks when in use.

The reservoir you will be using in this method should have a lid and be insulated so you can control the temperature of your nutrient solution

Aeroponics

Aeroponic is a method of hydroponic growing that doesn't need any growing medium. The roots in this method hang in mid-air, which is kept at 100% humidity with a sprinkler that sprinkles most of the solution, enabling the plant to absorb the nutrient while oxygenated. This method can lead to faster growth (up to 10 times faster than soil) for your plants.

Continuous Flow Method

Continuous flow refers to the continuous flow of nutrients to the roots of a plant. This method involves the use of pipes with holes at the top where the potted plants are placed and constantly supplied nutrients to the root inside the tube.

After reading this chapter, it is certain that one can easily set up and start an indoor growing technique or method without much trouble. Hence, starting an indoor planting or growing is totally dependent on the technique you choose - this being either the soil growing method or the hydroponic method.

Stay with us as we delve deeper in the next chapter on the right nutrients and environment suitable for your indoor growing.

Chapter 6
Indoor growing. Nutrients and Environmental Factors

With all our discussions in the previous chapters, I am certain you can now create an ideal environment and provide the right nutrients for your cannabis plant. The growing success and failure of your plant is totally dependent on you as a gardener, because you have the ability to fully control the environment and the number of nutrients provided to the plant.

We will be discussing in this chapter two major factors that are essential and contribute greatly to the development and growth of your marijuana.

Nutrient Factors

We have come to understand that nutrients are one of the most important factors needed for your cannabis cultivation to strive, grow, and develop into a healthy plant. These nutrients are classified into three categories.

The first category is the basic nutrients, otherwise known as the primary nutrients. These nutrients are Nitrogen (N) Phosphorus (P) and Potassium (K), or NPK as popularly called. We have talked about these three basic nutrients in previous chapters and come to the conclusion that they are instrumental to the survival or death of your cannabis plant.

The next category of nutrients found in the soil is secondary nutrients, or supplements as they are sometimes called. Secondary nutrients are also found in the soil, but in some cases, not all of these three supplements are present. These supplements are Calcium (Ca), Magnesium (Mg) and Sulphur (S). They also contribute immensely to the growth of your cannabis plant such that if any of the supplements are missing in the soil composition, it could lead to a deficiency in your plant's nutrition.

The last category of nutrients found in the soil is micronutrients. They are seven in number, namely: Zinc, Manganese, Iron, Boron, Copper, Molybdenum and Chlorine. These micronutrients don't have much effect on the good health and growth of your marijuana plant and problems of micronutrients hardly come up except there is a chemical reaction between the nutrients in the soil. This situation is referred to as a Lockout. Lockout takes place when a large percentage of one particular nutrient is being applied to your plant. This act can cause an imbalance between the nutrients and lock out other nutrients from being used. When this happens, your soil will need to be flushed.

In a situation where your soil faces nutrient deficiency, probably as a result of your plant absorbing most of the nutrients, the best solution to tackle this is feeding your plant.

Feeding

Feeding in this case has to do with refilling the soil with missing nutrients that have been absorbed by the marijuana plant. Feeding should only occur when your plant actually needs to be fed. In most cases, feeding your marijuana plant is done after 14 days at less than 50% of what is written on the nutrient label, in order to avoid plant burns. This is because marijuana plants easily experience burns, even with a small amount of nutrient feed. For instance, if you read on the label of the nutrient feed that you should use one full cap to 3 large gallons of water, you are advised to therefore use one full cap to 6 gallons of water.

Throughout the life cycle of your marijuana plant, you are expected to use only three solutions to feed your plants. These solutions are

1. A nutrient feed solution that has equal NPK or a solution that has more N over P and K. This solution is used in the vegetation growth stage of your cannabis plant.

2. A nutrient feed solution that has more P over N and K. It is used in the flowering stage of your plant.

3. A third nutrient solution is a solution that contains the secondary nutrients.

Note that secondary nutrients or supplements should be added every three weeks.

Air

Fresh air is essential in the healthy growth of a marijuana plant, especially when the plant is in the vegetative and flowering stages. Do not forget that there will come a time when your cannabis plant will experience dry periods in order for its roots to breathe. This just shows you how important fresh air is to your marijuana. Be sure to always open your windows for fresh air as it is the best option for your plants.

In winter, though, open your window for just 15 to 20 minutes to avoid freezing and stunted growth; and if you are growing in an enclosed area, be sure to create a good fanning system where your plants can get refreshed air. This can be done by using two fans, one to extract old air and the other to provide refreshed air.

Humidity

Humidity is simply the percentage of water available in the air. 40 to 80% relative humidity is what is best for your marijuana plant. Do not use equipment like a dehumidifier to control the humidity level of your grow room except if you are running a large operation. Be sure to always use fresh air to control and maintain the humidity level.

Temperature

The temperature of your grow room also has an influence on the healthy growth of your cannabis, hence the need for natural sunlight or a heating unit. Household temperature is therefore acceptable to grow cannabis in.

It is important to know the temperature that is suitable for your plants. Therefore, you have to learn to control the temperature level of your grow room. The best way to measure your grow room temperature is the use of the human body. If your grow room is too cold for you, then it's certainly too cold for your plants and therefore not suitable to grow your cannabis in. So it is advisable to utilize a thermometer in determining the temperature of the room just like the human body. Warm room temperature of about 75 degrees Fahrenheit should be the ideal target for your grow room. Therefore, when the room is too hot, open the windows or turn on the fan. When it's too cold, turn on the heater.

Fan

There is so much emphasis placed on the use of fan especially when you are practicing indoor growing. The slight, fresh breeze produced by the fan is important because it adds strength to the branches and stems of your cannabis plant. It also gives an outdoor feel to your indoor grow room.

Carbon Dioxide (CO_2)

During photosynthesis, plants take in CO_2 and release O_2, but there is no balance between the intake and release of the two elements, because the CO_2 is essential to the survival of your plant and helps the plant grow bigger buds. It is advisable that you as a grower use a carbon dioxide generator to increase your plant intake of CO_2.

Environmental Factors

Environmental factors have to do with controlling and maintaining the soil and pH level of your plants. These factors also influence the success and growth of your marijuana plants.

Soil Control

Soil control has to do with the removal of waste materials added to the soil by the cannabis plant and the addition of nutrients that have been absorbed by the cannabis plant. This process can lead to fluctuation thereby decreasing and increasing the pH level of the soil. Now it is up to you as a grower to maintain the pH level to seven or neutral in order to avoid an acidic or alkaline soil. This process is better known as soil control.

pH Control

pH control has to do with checking and maintaining the pH level of your soil to always be neutral. We have stated in previous chapters that when the pH of soil goes a bit lower or higher than seven (neutral), your soil pH needs adjusting. Therefore, it is advisable to check the pH level of your soil once a week or two days after feeding your cannabis plants.

One of the best ways to adjust your soil pH level when it has moved from being neutral (7) to acidic or alkaline is by using certain ingredients to bring the soil pH back to its normal level or engaging in a process called soil flush.

Bringing the pH Level to Neutral

This method consists of two processes: the bringing of the pH level from acidic to neutral and from alkaline to neutral. This method involves a lot of trials, mistakes, and errors, but this shouldn't stop you from experimenting. Some of the advanced cannabis growers today got where they are by a lot of experimenting and making mistakes. This method also helps you know and understand the number of ingredients and nutrients to add to your plants over time.

Also, note that your soil outcome after using this method will become impeccable.

1.Acidic to Neutral

Bringing a soil's pH level from acidic to neutral has to do with the use of lime. Apply lime to the affected soil consistently, especially after watering the plant. As you apply constantly, the quantity of the lime you apply should reduce so the pH level reaches a neutral level where you eventually stop the application.

Be sure to constantly use a pH meter to measure the pH level as you apply the lime.

2.Alkaline to Neutral

To bring a soil pH from alkaline to neutral, you need to make the soil more acidic; and this can be done by adding certain ingredients to the soil. These are:

1. Ground coffee
2. Lemon peel
3. Cottonseed meal
4. Acidic fertilizers

This method involves moderately adding any of the above ingredients until the soil eventually reaches a neutral level.

The products a lot of people, especially growers, are using today as a pH agent to adjust soil pH level is **pH up** and **pH down**. They are very effective and are available in different grow shops around.

Soil Flush

A soil flush is not highly recommended, but only ideal when your soil is experiencing serious fluctuations in pH level or when your plants experience serious burns caused by chemicals. It is highly advisable to mix raw nutrient feeds with water before using them on your plants, to avoid situations that will lead to soil flush.

Soil flush is usually a last resort and can be done in 3 different methods.

1. This method involves tilting your plant and pouring out the unwanted liquid.
2. This method is recommended for plants with perforated pots. In this case, you are expected to pour in plenty of water into the top of your pot and wait till

the water flushes out from the holes at the bottom of the pot.

3. This method is highly recommended for plants without perforated pots. Either you create a perforated pot by drilling holes underneath it and follow the second method or you carry out a transplant immediately to new soil.

With knowledge and research, you do not need an expert to help you check the nutrient and environmental factors of your plants or even your grow room. Keep reading through the next chapter and be enlightened on how flowering and breeding works in a marijuana plant.

Chapter 7
Indoor Growing: Flowering and Breeding

If you have been consistently following all our discussions in the previous chapters, I am sure you have been able to set up a convenient and healthy environment for your marijuana plant. At this point, you should have a grow room with conducive fresh air, plants in pots under grow lights, balance in soil nutrients and pH, adjusted lights, flat and stretched out leaves, and finally an increase in the height of your plants.

If you have not been able to achieve some of this, you shouldn't worry, mistakes are inevitable and they only make you more knowledgeable in your field. So moving on, if you have noticed some of the above traits like flat and stretched out leaves and increase in plant size, be sure to note that the next thing to follow is the stoppage in the growth of your plant and the development of new growth on your plants, especially between the stem and branches.

Do not panic when you see this happening. This period in the life cycle of your marijuana plants is known as the end of vegetation and pre-flowering stage respectively. In order words, the end of vegetation is the growth stoppage of the marijuana plant and the pre-flowering stage is the period where the development of new growth on the marijuana plant takes place. This new growth will eventually produce more leaves, flowers, and branches.

Pre-Flowering

At this stage of pre-flowering, you should hope your plant produces more females than males and you will be able to tell the sex of your plants by using three major methods. These methods are not 100% accurate in the reveal of the sex of your plants but sometimes they serve as reliable indicators. These methods are:

1. First Early Sexing Method

The first early sexing method is applicable when you are growing all your seeds at the same time. When these seeds start growing, then you will be able to tell the sex of the plants by observing their heights. The taller ones are male while the much shorter plants are female.

Another thing to note in this method is that the male plants tend to start pre-flowering before the female plants. So when you notice a tall plant that started pre-flowering before the short plants, be sure to know it's a male plant and vice versa.

2. Second early sexing method

The second early sexing method has to do with checking the calyx of the plant by using magnifying glasses. Now if you notice that the calyx is raised on a stem then it should be a male plant but if the calyx (new growth) is not raised on the stem then it is likely to be a female plant.

3. Third early sexing method

This third early sexing method is known as force-flowering a cutting. It is the best method out there you can use to determine the sex of your plant in an early stage. This method involves cutting a piece of your plant and placing it in a cup of water or cloning medium like Rockwool for 24 hours.

In this 24 hours, provide your plant with 12 hours of light and 12-hour darkness.

The result of this method will be a flower displayed by the cutting. This flower will reveal the sex of the plant. If you end up using a cloning medium, then the result will be an exact clone that consists of similar genes and sex as the plant it was cut from, hence revealing the sex of the original plants it was cut from.

Like I said earlier, these methods are not seen as 100 % accurate and should not be totally relied on. These methods are advantageous as they help you understand differences between the male and female plants.

Pre-Flowering Period

The pre-flowering period of a cannabis plant is usually one or two weeks. In this period, the calyx region of the plant begins to take different shape and size based on its sex. It is during this period when the calyx is taking different shapes that you can fully determine your plant's sex.

Facts About Growing Cannabis

Making certain decisions sometimes can be difficult and without proper advice or research, you might end up making a decision that will affect you negatively. So, before you decide whether to flower your plants or continue vegetative growth, here are some interesting facts about growing cannabis that you should consider:

1. Some cannabis plants have a very long life cycle and can survive up to 10 years by just being under steady light at all times. Over this long period of time, the plant reaches its maximum height, stops producing branches, and eventually starts to turn to a bush. The rest of its life cycle will be focused on replacing old leaves by growing new ones.

2. Another interesting fact to note is that bud production is actually not equivalent to the height of your plants, rather it is equivalent to your strain's genes, the number of nodes your plant has, and your growing environment. It is also important to note that all plants' node areas will eventually turn to a budding area and every strain has the potential to produce buds.

3. Also, flowering a plant immediately after it has matured tends to increase the production of buds, especially if the plants are plenty, rather than the extended vegetative growth. In other words, the shorter option tends to produce more turnover in buds than the extensive option.

Flower Time

If your plants manage to reach the pre-flowering stage, it means your plants have matured enough to begin flowering. Now the most important question to ask is if you, as a grower, want to take a long route by continuing with vegetative growth or start flowering.

If you choose to take the long route, then you have to make provision for a bigger grow room because the cannabis plant tends to increase over time in height and width.

On the other hand, if you choose to flower your plants, then the best option is to utilize a 12/12 schedule for your cannabis plant.

The 12/12 Schedule

The 12/12 schedule promotes great outcomes and good quality buds for your cannabis plants.

This schedule has to do with providing your plant with the natural 12 hours of light and 12-hour darkness that a full 24 hour day provides. If you are using an indoor grow method, it is therefore important to switch on your lights for 12 hours and switch them off for another 12 hours.

This, therefore, gives your plant a natural stimulation to produce a flower. As you continue to keep up with this 12/12 schedule, your plants will continue to be plentiful with flowers, which is exactly what we seek as growers.

Also, note that for the success of this 12/12 schedule you are expected to commit fully to these routines. For the 12 hour darkness, be sure not to let any single light penetrate through the darkness because it can affect the plant's flowering process. In other words, your grow room should be totally and completely sealed from light. You can use a photographer's darkroom as an inspiration for creating your grow room.

12/12 Schedule Problems

If you start using the 12/12 schedule before your plants reach the pre-flowering stage, then you might face two major problems:

1. Sex problems caused by sex (the issue of hermaphrodite)
2. Abnormal bud growth.

Breeding

If you really want to start breeding your own cannabis strain, but you find scientific write-ups highly confusing, and graphs and punnett squares put you to sleep, then this is the handbook for you. We will break down how to breed your own special strains with more than enough traits to help them out in severe weather conditions.

Breeding cannabis and continuing a lineage in the seed is not a must for a grower. However, indoor growers that have acquired high-level cultivation skills and mastered the essential techniques can most definitely become interesting breeders. Creating hybrids is also achievable even at a first trial. Most of the cannabis strains that have become legend were created by home growers, even by accident.

While it might not be possible to build your own seed bank from the grow tent in the spare bedroom, small-scale breeding is the next best thing to do. The good news is that you don't need a master's degree in botany to pull this off. Just the normal and ordinary good old-fashioned dope growing experience will suffice. Thus, this is how to go about it.

Same Strain Breeding

Now, this is very easy. Breeding from a same batch or strain can be quite intriguing. Get a male and a female cannabis plant in the same batch, then crossbreed them. For example, if you are familiar with the strain and cropping from the same pack of seeds, you can potentially select a breeding pair to cross.

This is an old-school dope growers' process mostly applied outdoors. Although, breeding from the same batch has potential indoors, provided the original organic seeds are genuine. If so, not only will the resulting progeny be more or less stable but you will have saved cash on seeds for the next crop. Breeding from a reliable batch is a good introduction to cannabis breeding.

Poly hybrids

Ever heard of breeding two different strains to produce outstanding results? Well, a poly hybrid is the crossing of two commercial, unrelated varieties. To begin with, this will not be entirely stable, and won't produce genuine F1 hybrids. Results will undoubtedly be mixed, but poly hybrids are pretty vigorous and winning pheno's can be found in them.

F1 Hybrids

These amazing, genuine F1 Hybrids are the jewels in the crown of the Royal Queen Seeds catalog. The cold, hard truth is that creating fantastically potent, productive and vigorous growing F1 hybrids is a long-term process. It is not child's play, either. It involves lots of processes and procedures. Professional breeders invest years of their lives into breeding projects and select cultivars from hundreds if not thousands of cannabis plants.

F1 hybrids can only be derived from crossing pedigree stabilized or landrace strains. They express genuine hybrid vigor. Unless you're planning a strain-hunting expedition, tracking down heirloom landrace seeds is hard graft. It's probably more convenient to stick with the RQS catalog for awesome hybrids.

Similarly, filial breeding can be complicated. Honestly, it's far too demanding for the first time home breeder. By crossing a pair of F1s (first generation) the resulting progeny is the F2 (second generation). Unfortunately, these seeds will be far less stable and far more difficult to work with than the previous F1 generation.

Careful selective breeding in large numbers is required to succeed with this approach. Often it takes multiple generations of breeding, perhaps until F5 (fifth generation) or even F6 (sixth generation) before the line can be stabilized. That is how much stress the F1 hybrids involve.

We believe this chapter must have opened up your eyes and mind to the terms "flowering" and "breeding" in the cannabis plant. So, instead of surfing the net or a scientific jargon to look for answers you might not find, this handbook will further broaden your horizon in our next chapter.

Chapter Eight
Indoor Growing: Maintaining the Marijuana Plant

Always remember that making mistakes while growing the cannabis plant is very normal. Don't push yourself too hard in order to achieve your desired result. Beginners have a long history of messing things up. There's a learning curve for every activity, and growing marijuana is no different. People who have been growing weed for 20 years are naturally going to be a lot better at it than those who have just decided to start. But, most newbies might be dissuaded from trying it because they fear humiliation or failure.

However, don't let that dissuade you no matter what. Rome wasn't built in one day. Window growing won't cut it most of the time. Despite the fact that the best source of light for any plant is the sun, growing them indoors and using the window as your only light source is a bad way to go.

When it comes to indoor growing, marijuana plants need as much light as you can give them. While it might be cheaper to just try to use the sun, it won't be effective. Buy lights if you're growing indoors. Be prepared. Growing marijuana comes with a lot of vagaries that can leave you feeling overwhelmed. There are also plenty of things that you should just be prepared for.

The plants need water, nutrients, light, and CO2 (not exactly in that order). But, plants can also be hit with a bug infestation, lack of nutrient quality, and inadequate amounts of CO2. Make sure you have a contingency plan ready in the event that the plants start to exhibit negative signs.

Use the right fertilizer. Many beginners might just grab any old fertilizer at the garden store. While the plants will grow, they won't thrive like you want them to. Most fertilizers have an NPK ratio conveniently displayed on the bag or another packaging. This isn't just another irrelevant mathematical term, though. It describes the concentration of nitrogen (N), phosphorus (P), and potassium (K) in relation to one another.

For every growth period (excluding flowering), you'll want to use a fertilizer that is higher in nitrogen than anything else. During flowering, the fertilizer should have more phosphorus. Just because the soil is natural doesn't mean it will work. Many new marijuana growers automatically think that any outdoor soil will provide ample nutrients for their plants. In reality, that soil could be nothing more than glorified dirt.

It could also be too acidic or too alkaline and won't even help germinate the seeds properly. When growing outdoors, always infuse the soil with some fertilizer or another potting mix. Also, make sure to test the pH balance to ensure that it's as close to the middle (7.0) as possible.

Be active. As you might have already guessed, growing marijuana is not a passive expenditure of your time. These plants need to be cared for almost like they are your children (however ridiculous that might sound). They have remarkably short lifespans from germination to harvest, but you can't just plant them and hope for the best.

Trim them, prune them, feed them, water them, pamper them, and make sure they're getting enough light, CO_2, and ventilation.

Mistakes To Avoid When Growing Marijuana:

Don't let the plants get rootbound. One thing that many beginners might not know is that marijuana roots grow incredibly fast. When they are in a container, the roots generally line the walls of that container and reach to the bottom.

If the container is too small, they can get rootbound. They will also die. Make sure you (carefully) transplant the plants from smaller containers into larger ones after they've exhibited some accelerated growth (from seedling to vegetative state).

Don't get crazy with pruning. You may have heard that pruning a plant increases growth. You may have also heard that more pruning correlates to further growth. While that can be true, there's no need to prune down an entire marijuana plant. You'll just end up weakening it and potentially killing it if you go too far.

Don't panic. Most of the problems that occur with plants are the result of easily reversible mistakes. For instance, if some of the leaves start to turn yellow and the plant starts to wilt, it could just be lacking in one particular nutrient. Some leaves on the plant will also just die either because of a lack of light or because of natural processes. In general, it's not indicative of a greater problem throughout the plant.

Maintaining the Indoor Cannabis Garden also costs much more money than you might possibly bargain for. It is important to know that almost everything the plant needs is artificial and costs money. From the soil to the pot, the light, the air, and so much more - it all costs money.

Therefore, it is advisable to know what you are getting into before determining whether you are cool with it or not. Maintaining the indoor plant also means checking the plants and the facilities you have in place, so as to be sure if they are perfect and in good shape

Indoor growing also comes with its own fair share of pests. There are lots of pests that would attack the plants if you don't maintain and care for them. Here are some of the deadly pests you should watch out for:

1. Spider Mites
2. Aphids

3. Cabbage Looper
4. Squash Bugs
5. Potato Beetles

Some growers choose to use harsh synthetic chemicals like pesticides and fungicides to keep their plants free of pests. Although these chemical agents might do their job, they also cause great harm to human and environmental health. Residue from these products can even end up in your smoking stash. Thus, the best way to stop these pests from killing your plant is through biological means.

For example, growing some beneficial plants very close to your cannabis plant will help push off the pests of the cannabis plant. Their aroma, scent, and way of growing will help put a stop to the pests eating up your cannabis. There are also some beneficial insects which help eat up the pest that eats up your plant. For example, the spider spins its web around the plants to catch other insects that are pests to your plants. Grow flowers around your weed so they can attract spiders.

Be that as it may, maintaining your indoor plant is paramount for their healthy growth. Focus your attention on how best you can care and maintain your plants. You will be glad about the outcome in the long run.

Chapter Nine
Outdoor Growing: Where and How?

Outdoor growing is different. Unlike the popular indoor growing method which entails growing the cannabis plant in a secluded area of the building (grow room), outdoor growing of the cannabis plant takes courage and guts to pull off successfully. You can't just start sowing cannabis in your background because of the immense land you have in your compound. The outdoor growing of the plant needs planning and strategy.

Most outdoor growers are people with much confidence, self-esteem, and good connections. A single individual cannot just wake up one day and start cultivating cannabis in the open. There are lots of people and processes that must be followed. For example, you will need people to help secure your investment; people to help cater for the plants.

In this line of business or hobby, no one can live the life of complete autarky. However, regardless of how or where you want to begin your outdoor growing, you must first make a decision in your mind about treading this path. Are you well equipped? Are you truly ready? Do you have what it takes? Are all conditions and factors met? If yes, then this chapter will fuel you up with ideas on how to go about it.

Don't get it twisted, outdoor growing and indoor growing of the plant are two sides of the same coin. Simply put, they are different roads that lead to the same destination – cultivating and harvesting good, healthy cannabis plants. They are distinctive, yet geared towards the achievement of the same goal.

The outdoor growing of the cannabis plant is the traditional way of growing cannabis. Before the prohibition placed on the psychoactive herb, growers of the cannabis plant enjoyed complete freedom. Outdoor growing was the order of the day amongst growers of the plant. But currently, that freedom has been cut short.

Outdoor growers now carry out their hobbies in absolute secrecy for the fear of being persecuted, arrested, and jailed. Therefore, if I want to grow cannabis outdoors, I would put it at the back of my mind that this line of business or venture is a very risky one. To this effect, I wouldn't want to jeopardize it in any way whatsoever.

I would find a suitable and conducive place where my cannabis plants would thrive. I would block all possible obstacles that would present themselves as a stumbling block to the success of my outdoor garden.

As an outdoor grower, we often do not feel like we have tied up loose ends, even if we have put in place one of the best security systems one can possibly imagine. We often feel jittery and scared, always feeling like we are being watched with a keen eye. What if we are caught? What if the security is just not enough? These and more are the questions that might keep going through our minds.

But at the end of it all, we realize that we were just being paranoid over nothing. Ease your mind, boost your confidence, and have self-esteem. Remember, it's what you love doing. Nevertheless, all our plans and strategies would be wasted if we didn't find the right place for our outdoor growing.

Finding the Right Place

Like we said above, you just can't wake up one morning and start sowing cannabis anywhere you want. Sounds absurd, isn't it? There are lots of factors to consider when it comes to finding the right place to plant your cannabis, especially with outdoor growing.

1. **Tightly Secured Environment:** Security is one of the key ingredients of any establishment. Be it an investment, a parastatal or, as in this case, an outdoor growing farm. There should be laid down processes, structures, and arrangements which provide top-notch security over the garden. For example, a sudden surge that suddenly occurs in the amount of electric current used within a short time would definitely attract unwanted attention from the relevant authorities.

   Also, an increase in the water bill can charge up interest from other authorities. How would you settle those issues? What necessary arrangements have you fashioned to tackle this breach? These and more are relevant questions you should ask yourself.

Finding the right place for outdoor growing of your cannabis plant is no small task. Ensuring maximum security is of utmost importance. In other words, the site must be tightly secured. It must be away from the public eye.

2. **Large Area of Land:** An outdoor growing area needs to be spacious. The grow space must be large enough to accommodate all seedlings. Unlike with indoor growing where seedlings are housed inside a building with air, water, and light provided artificially to ensure good yields, outdoor growing is just natural.

Natural soil, natural air, and natural light directly from the sun; all these can be achievable with a large area of land. It creates space for the seedlings to spread out and reach their peak. To this effect, the seedlings won't be competing for nutrients, air, water, and light to survive.

3. **Good Climate:** According to research, a good climate condition is vital for the growth of a healthy cannabis plant. These climate conditions which are not too hot or too cold provide the plant with a perfect means of reaching its best height. A study conducted in this field has shown that a climate condition which can sustain the tomato plant would also sustain the cannabis plant.

According to the study, tomatoes and weed were planted alongside each other and the results were very encouraging. They both excelled in that particular weather condition. Thus, wherever you can grow tomatoes, you can grow cannabis, too. In choosing where to start your outdoor cannabis farm, putting the climate condition into consideration is vital. You don't want to grow your plant in a harsh environment.

4. **Good Soil:** First thing first, looking for a place with very fertile and healthy soil to grow your cannabis plant is of utmost importance. And if the soil is not treated before planting, we would advise you do so before starting your cultivation.

Additionally, you want to remove as many weeds as possible. These weeds can compete with your plants for nutrients if left alone, thereby making them grow weak, unhealthy, and withered. All the above-listed points are vital to finding the right place for your outdoor growing area.

The security of the place must be guaranteed. Even when the authorities pull unnecessary and unexpected stunts, there should be arrangements laid down to checkmate these stunts. A wide area of land, a good climate condition, and a nutritious soil should also be the key factors towards choosing where to sow your cannabis seeds outdoors.

How to Sow Cannabis Outdoors

The outdoor growing of the cannabis plant can be quite fun, especially if it involves more than one person. A lot of cannabis smokers out there would easily agree with us that outdoor cannabis is the best of them all. Many of them even went ahead to describe the outdoor cannabis as the perfect weed, with a scintillating scent they just can't resist.

This should tell you a lot about outdoor growing cannabis. With the right place to sow, the right weather conditions, and perfect security, there is nothing stopping you from burying the seed in the ground. Well, except one question; how do you go about it?

You have a plot of land already? That is just perfect. Start by treating the ground. It is important to note that untreated ground ends up producing very low yield or harvest. It is also prone to pests and small predators ready to reduce your hard work to nothing. Therefore, for much better yields and harvests, we would recommend you start treating your land henceforth.

Remove all disturbing weeds you can find. Weeds can be very stubborn most times. To this effect, you shouldn't relent even after removing them totally. They have the tendency to come back even stronger and thicker. Make sure you don't get lazy when it comes to weeding out your farm. Employ any technique you can think of, so long you don't end up hurting your plant.

Don't leave the weeds around carelessly for people to see. This may attract unwanted attention and attractions from passers-by. Tie them in a sack if you must or dispose of them far away from the farm. Afterward, sowing your cannabis seeds should come next. A lot of people end up making the mistake of sowing the seeds too deep.

If you are one of those people, then please stop. Here is why! When the seeds go much deeper than expected, it ends up taking more time to sprout or they even might end up not growing at all. Adding pre-made soil with an NPK value won't be a bad idea at all. Getting the pre-made soil should be easy as they can be found at the nearest store close to you.

This is where continuous weeding comes into play. Week in week out, weed out any form of obstruction till your seeds germinate into seedlings. Don't forget to sprinkle water every now and then, if you have to. Growing cannabis outdoors is as easy as that.

Like we discussed earlier, there is nothing new about cannabis planting, however, knowing how to plant the seeds appropriately, knowing where to plant, and ensuring some safety measures are taken towards the protection of your cannabis plant is paramount. The next chapter will delve into the outdoor planting techniques. You don't want to miss it!

Chapter Ten
Outdoor Growing: Planting and Planting Techniques

Outdoor growing differs from the indoor method of growing as well as in its planting techniques and styles. A grower who wants to adopt the outdoor growing method would not use the indoor growing techniques, and vice versa. The end result is bound to be disappointing, disappointing, and degrading in the long run.

Where indoor growing of the cannabis plant uses artificial lights and air, outdoor growing of the plant doesn't really need the artificial setup. Imagine installing the light and air conditioning equipment outside. Crazy, isn't it? That is one of the reasons why lots of expert growers prefer using the outdoor growing to the indoor counterpart.

Growing cannabis outdoors is a lot cheaper than indoors. When it rains, it's free and natural water to your plants. When the sun shines, it's free of charge - without cost. Even the air the plants take in is totally free. That way, you spend less when compared to Indoor growing. However, you can decide to use a grow pot outdoors.

Grow pots come with their advantages and disadvantages. Inasmuch as they can be moved about easily while changing positions and postures of the plants, they are very advantageous. However, the negative part of the movable outdoor grow pot is that they sometimes deny the plant good light, the great nutrients they could get when planted on an unlimited space, and the good air they would get when outdoors.

To get the best out of your cannabis plants, one must learn the necessary planting techniques and know exactly how to apply these techniques at the right times. As a beginner, these esteemed techniques, skills, or styles might be news to you. If you find yourself in this category, don't feel bad. There is always a first time for everything. Even the expert growers out there started out as beginners.

Thus, with time, as you would expand your knowledge and learn these unique techniques, you would find it very easy and entertaining as you apply them. To that effect, this chapter would go a long way in opening your eyes to the advanced techniques you can use to upgrade and increase the yields or harvests of your plant.

These techniques come with both indoor and outdoor growing but are more synonymous to outdoor growing. This chapter will broaden your horizon on the positive side of these techniques before applying them. Growing is very easy. Sometimes all we need to do is to bury a seed and pretend to forget it even exists.

Like we said earlier, planting techniques are very much advanced in their procedures and processes. They go beyond the normal procedure we discussed in the previous chapter. Exercising these techniques on your farm would not only result in a better output or harvest but also better cannabis efficacy and genetics.

This would go a long way in ensuring and improving the qualities of the plant's bud cultivation. Get a handbook, if you must. Ask a friend or two to teach you how to apply them, if it comes to that.

Planting Techniques

All planting techniques are unique. But the good news is you can use two or more of them at the same time. They complement one another.

1. **Thinning:** Thinning is mostly synonymous with outdoor growers. Imagine growing your weed from inception in an orderly and uniform manner, only for them to start growing shabbily and aggressively or even out of line. What would you have done? One would notice that some of the plants are growing faster than others, racing toward the light.

   In this case, adjusting the light to suit other plants would be the best thing to do, or better still, moving and switching the plants is also great. Spacing also comes to play here. However, if even after adjusting the light and the space between the plants, your plants still grow abnormally, thinning is the next thing you should consider.

   The racing plants tend to draw closer toward the light at the expense of the others. Therefore, other plants that don't get much light end up growing slowly, shorter, and abnormally. Thinning these racy plants becomes paramount so as to give room for other plants to absorb the sunlight.

Cut them down, trim them, pare down, or clip them to the normal size of the deprived plants. Trust me, when all plants are of uniform height, they will thrive together in harmony. The end result will be bumper harvests and surplus yields.

2. **Cloning:** Ever heard of the term cloning? I'm sure what is going through your mind right now is the duplication and replication of a phenomenon, person, or something. Well, you are right. However, cannabis plant cloning doesn't mean the plant would be taken to a lab and be put through lots of chemical processes just to get a replica. It is simply the planting of unwanted plants you removed earlier in your farm.

Do you remember those unwanted parts of your plants you thinned out? Yes, those parts! Why throw them away when they can be planted again? The act of planting those unwanted plants is called cloning. A lot of growers end up throwing the thinned plants away. But rest assured, by the time you are done with thinning your plant, there will be more than enough space for you to clone. To this effect, your harvest will increase drastically.

3. **Plant Shifting:** This type of growing technique is applicable to mostly outdoor pot growers. Like we

discussed earlier, some plants have the tendency to grow faster than the rest. Thus, growing towards the light. This is a hindrance to other plants as they may end up not getting enough light.

Thinning would be the best solution but some growers don't like thinning. They believe that thinning slows down their cannabis growing process. Be that as it may, switching the plants becomes paramount. Interchange the position of the faster-growing plants with the slow ones. This should regulate the growth and size of the plants. And trust me, the slow-growing plant will catch up in no time.

Notwithstanding, if your plants cannot be switched from one place to another, try other means. For instance, in the hydroponics style of planting cannabis might be very difficult to move from one place to another. Therefore, using another means of moving the plants like tying a rope to the fast-growing plants in a straight form also works just fine.

For outdoor cannabis plants, you can use sticks, bamboos, and stakes with a very long, thick thread to hold the plants in an upright position. Exercise the planting technique when the need arises and watch your harvest quadruple.

4. **Pruning:** Do you often wonder how some of your friend's cannabis plants end up getting more than one flower at the top colas? I'm sure you must be thinking

your plant is growing abnormally. That is not true. As a matter of fact, your friends exercised a planting technique which they obviously didn't want to let you in on.

This technique is called pruning. At the 3rd or 4th week of vegetation growth, the top should be pruned off from the stem, which will give the main stem an opportunity to sprout in two or more directions. It no longer takes the normal straight shape but a remarkable "V" shape.

Nevertheless, this technique does not always work out all the time. The plant's response to the technique depends solely on its strain and surroundings. Topping off a plant sometimes produces more than five top colas. Some Cannabis strains also reach their maximum bud production only if they are topped off. In other words, pruning leads to more bud production and more bud production equals bumper harvest.

With everything we've discussed above, increasing your yields and harvest shouldn't be hard to pull off. From the life cycle of the marijuana plant to its germination, indoor and outdoor growing, factors that may influence growing marijuana, and so much more.

All these should give you more than enough ideas on how to go about establishing your own private cannabis garden. The questions now remain: Do I really have what it takes? Can I actually pull this off? Growing marijuana can be very addictive. Far more addictive than its content (Note:

Marijuana does not contain any addictive content but the love of growing it can be very addictive).

To many people, it is the hobby in which they derive utmost pleasure and contentment. It is far more than just a business venture even for those who commercialize growing cannabis. Growing marijuana is rewarding in the long run.

To this effect, using planting techniques on your cannabis plant would not only increase yields and harvest, but it will also ensure that cannabis growing outdoors is much more rewarding than its indoor counterpart. These advanced techniques would give order and uniformity to your plants. Quite rewarding, isn't it?

These diverse techniques are different paths that lead to one destination – a great harvest. Therefore, we would advise you to be like your friends. Apply these techniques where they are meant to be applied and of course, appropriately. The joy of all cannabis growers, expert and beginner, is to see their plants blossom. Don't be left out.

Chapter Eleven
Outdoor Growing: Care of the Growing Plants

Jamie was very passionate about his cannabis plants. Every morning, he would weed, water, and check his cannabis plants just to be completely sure they were in good shape. As a key follower of the Growing Marijuana Handbook, he always made sure he followed the handbook to the letter. Thus, he continued the processes as outlined by the book.

This process continued until Jamie traveled for a business trip out of town for two weeks. Before leaving, he had checked with his friend Sam to help care for his precious plants. Sam wasn't Jamie, thus he would forget to check the plants frequently. Day in day out, the plants continued to wither away due to Sam's negligence.

They continued dying off with pests and smaller predators perching on the leaves, branches, buds, stems, flowers, and trims. This was solely because Sam didn't pay much attention to the care of his friend's precious plants.

Now let's imagine you were Jamie. How would you feel after coming back from a long distance journey, tired and weary, only to see your precious plants reduced to rubbish? Unimaginable, right? To this effect, we would advise you care for your plants yourself. No one takes care of a property more than the owner. Leave no one in charge!

But if you must, then always check in with the person frequently. Knowing how to grow cannabis, even in some spectacular way, is not enough. It is important to note that even as you become an expert grower, knowing all the techniques and strategies towards growing healthy cannabis, if you don't take care of your plant, it's going to be a wasted effort. A healthy cannabis plant can be only produced via care and attention given to it from the seedling stage to the harvesting stage.

Care of the plant means you nurture, nourish, and sustain the quality, quantity, and caliber of the cannabis species you are growing. Sometimes, even the sight of our outdoor cannabis farm scares us. With the large area of land, we begin to imagine where we would even start from. If it's weeding, then weed early and weed frequently. That way, the weeds won't get to encroach on the plants.

Care of the plants takes various procedures and processes. They vary from the kind of growth you adopt. In other words, indoor growing care is totally unique from that of outdoor growing. This can be because of their indoor and outdoor features. For example, due to the large space provided by Mother Nature, the outdoor cannabis plant care includes weeding out the large chunk of unwanted and irrelevant plants.

However, these unwanted plants are not present indoors as they can be hardly seen. This is because of the nature of planting indoor plants. Indoor plants also grow in a pot, box, and bucket. This gives them limited space to get entangled and spread their leaves and branches as far as they want

Care of the Growing Plants

1. **Weeding:** According to expert growers, the best and most convenient way to weed your cannabis plants is by hand. Also, regular growers tend to use killer weeds or weed killers, as the case may be, around their Cannabis plant. It is believed that these weed killers may have a negative effect on your cannabis plant if it's not applied carefully.

   However, the overall benefits of these weed killers on your plants cannot be overemphasized. We would recommend you first try it on your clones in order to test the effect it would have on the cannabis plant firsthand. Little wonder why weeding by hand is the preferable choice to the expert growers out there. It is, no doubt, the most acceptable method of weeding to date.

   Mother Nature often starts sprouting annoying weeds all over your cannabis plant farm. They even get to a point where they start getting intertwined with your plants, sucking and tapping off nutrients from the plant. You definitely can't remove the weed aggressively. You might end up affecting the cannabis plant.

   Thus, a careful weeding with your hands is the solution to that problem. A weeded area of plant ensures that the plants don't get to fight or compete for any nutrients, sunlight, air, and water. It paves way for the plants to grow healthy and reach their peak. A weeded cannabis plant benefits the plants immensely as they spread out without any form of obstruction or competition.

I guess you must be seeing the issue of weeding as a very demanding one. Well, not to worry. According to expert growers, weeding your growing plants need only be frequent during its first 2-3 weeks. To this effect, weeding is advised to be carried out every week. But after this stage, it can be done once a month until your plant reaches the harvest stage.

Nevertheless, if your area of land is densely populated with weeds, then weeding by hand or the use of weed killers becomes irrelevant and a total waste of time. Imagine weeding a hectare of land with your hands; absurd, isn't it? This is where ground covers come into play.

2. **Ground Cover:** Ground cover, as the name implies, is a kind of cover which is spread on the ground with different sizes of holes bored into it. These holes provide space for sowing your cannabis seeds. Ground covers can be anything that can be spread on the ground to stop the intrusion of a common weed. They can be plastic, bin liners, or even sheets of paper. It will definitely keep the weed down.

3. **Watering:** When it comes to outdoor growing of the cannabis plant, Mother Nature should be in charge of

watering the plants with her rain. It is her job as all your water should come from the sky. Hitherto, if the season changes from a raining season to a dry one, watering the plants yourself becomes paramount.

The kind of watering method or equipment you will use solely rests on the size of your farm. You certainly won't want to use a watering can to water a hectare of land. For a small area of land or even outdoor pots, you can use the watering can, a cup of water or even put water in a sack if the farm is a little bit far.

For a large area of land, expert growers make use of a sprinkler system. This is very fast and can reach other plants that are far apart. Like we said earlier, the size of your farm determines everything, which includes how much water to be sprinkled.

Some cannabis plants make use of more than one gallon of water per day, while some just need a cup of water. Knowing when the plants need water is paramount. The cannabis plant has the tendency to hold pockets of water below the surface. But how does one begin to tell which plant needs water and which one doesn't?

It's simple. Each cannabis plant tends to wilt badly when it is in dire need of water. Therefore, whenever you see your plants getting wilted, you now know the reason. Another way of knowing this is to keep a foot-deep hole beside your plant. Be very careful when doing this so as not to damage any vital roots.

Then proceed by feeling the soil with your hands. How moist is it? Is it completely dry? These are questions you would get your answers to, after feeling the soil.

4. **Safe from Predator and Pest:** There is absolutely no healthy plant without its fair share of this problem. Predators and pests eat through your plants until they die off. Without enough care, they will easily find a way into your plants, thereby reducing the quality, quantity, and caliber of your plants.

To salvage your plants from this path of destruction, one must do the needful. This may include using cut-throat measures and means to achieve your objectives. Expert growers have agreed that the number-one defense system one can use in eradicating these small predators is the cat. No small predator dares to enter the house of the cat, except for the cunning and daring ones. That will solve your problem on the predators.

For pest control, please ensure you use only pesticides that are labeled with "For Food Product Use." If you don't see this label on the pesticides, then do not use it on your plants. Follow the instructions and manuals of the breeder to the letter. You wouldn't want to get sick from taking in harmful cannabis.

Some of the pests and predators you might encounter include:

o Woodchucks: They bite off the stems, chunk after chunk, until they eventually fall off the plants. Use

- o predator urine or construct a meshwork fence around the plants.

- o Powder Bugs: They destroy the plants by constantly laying their eggs in the bud and stem. This will kill off your plants within the shortest possible time. Spray a Pyrethrum-based insecticide on your plants. This keeps them away.

- o Groundhogs: They continuously feed on your plant until it dies off. Get some dry chloride and apply it around their holes. This should keep them away.

- o Wilt Fungus: As the name implies, it wilts your precious plants completely. Gently apply the fungicide. You can find it in a store nearby. It works like magic.

- o White Flies: They are very deadly. Within days, they can destroy your plants, if given the chance. Ensure you get the original safer's soap. It is very potent in killing off the whitefly. It can be found at any grow shops close by.

Everything needs care and attention to be done or turn out perfectly. Else, they might fall through in the process. The same thing applies to the cannabis plant. Remember, it is your passion and hobby. Treat your plants with love, care, and attention - and watch them blossom. A lot of obstacles, factors, hindrance, and stumbling blocks could create problems for you along the line.

Potential problems abound, like pest and small predator issues, lack of nutrients in the soil, racing plants, abnormal growth, and so much more. It is your job to ensure each problem is taken care of adequately. Consult a friend if you must; read a book or surf the net if you have to. Lastly, no one takes care of the plant better than the grower.

Chapter Twelve
Outdoor Growing: Nutrients and Environmental Factors

In the previous chapters, we basically surfed through the processes and procedures of growing a cannabis plant. Most of the work and praises are heaped on these processes, but we must not neglect the important roles nutrients and environmental factors play in the healthy and rapid growth of the cannabis plant.

The soil contains major nutrients (Nitrogen, Phosphorus, and Potassium) which nurture the plant from its germination stage. These nutrients, which are also known as NPK, can either come with the soil or as a fertilizer. These nutrients come in equal proportions (20:20:20). The remaining 40 percent contains other elements and contents that make up the soil.

A soil without nutrients can be said to be a train without an engine. There will be no way the train will move. This same instance applies to the soil. There is no way the cannabis seeds will germinate with a soil that lacks nutrients. Please, always remember that each plant has a particular nutrient it wants more than the rest.

The cannabis plant wants more of the N (Nitrogen) and the normal amount of the P (Phosphorus) and K (Potassium) during vegetative growth. Additionally, during the flowering stage, use nutrients that are higher in the P (Phosphorus). Knowing all of this is of utmost importance for the growth of your cannabis plant.

The sun, air, and water also go a long way in nourishing your plants to a large extent. But with the addition of nutrients, it will only get better. Here are top nutrients you can add to your outdoor Cannabis farm;

1. **General Hydroponics Organic Go Box:** Sourced from botanical extracts and natural minerals, these organic nutrients will boost your plants with the necessary things needed for a healthy take off. These nutrients will provide additional support to the already existing nutrients. It supports the roots, makes the leaves look brighter and greener, and helps out in the different phases of the plant.

2. **Dyna-Gro8 oz Dyna GB8OZ Liquid Grow and Bloom:** This is a very good choice of products for all weed growers, both indoor and outdoor. You will find this product incredibly easy and convenient to use ahead of other products in this range. It provides the plant with all the necessary nutrients right from the beginning.

The Dyna-Gro Liquid Grow (80z) should be used first to boost the growth and size of the plants, while the Dyna-Gro Liquid Bloom (80z) should be used during the flowering stage. This will help bloom the flowers and buds into becoming much more effective, productive, and of great quality. It is perfect for beginners.

3. General Hydroponic 1 Quart GLCMBX009 Calimagic & Flora GRO, Micro & Bloom Combo: This is just the perfect fertilizer you need for correcting soil with a deficiency in potassium. It also boosts the rapid growth of a plant by giving it the necessary food for that. This particular nutrient has lots of important functions.

4. Espoma TR44-Pound Tree-Tone 6-3-2 Plant Food: There is no better natural food you can feed your plant aside this fertilizer. Tired of chemical-based fertilizers? Then try this natural fertilizer from Espoma. It contains a massive embodiment of over 13 nutrients which will nourish your weed. It can be used from the initial stage of germination until harvest.

5. Clonex Rooting Gel: Cloning is a technique used in planting thinned out plants. With Clonex, this thinned plants that are cloned will grow faster and better. The rooting gel works like magic by repairing, protecting, and stimulating the root growth of your cloned plants for a much better plant in the long run.

Environmental Factors

The environment is everything when it comes to planting cannabis. If you plant your cannabis in an environment that is not conducive, the results will most

The Growing Marijuana Handbook

definitely be bad. You can't expect your plants to grow perfectly in bad environmental conditions. These factors can deter, delay or even lead to damage of the plants in the long run. The environmental factors are complex. They are difficult to control and most times just simply out of our control.

1. **Land Management Practices:** This is an effective factor that influences the growth of outdoor marijuana. Land clearing, habitat fragmentation, and over-grazing help the growth of weed by providing the clones with a new area of land and ensure the weed doesn't have a strong competition with native vegetation.

2. Land management practices are activities which are carried out to improve the quality nutrients and fertility of the land. To this effect, the marijuana plant gets the necessary nutrients it needs from the soil.

3. **Natural Disasters:** As we discussed earlier, growing outdoor weed comes with lots of factors. Natural disasters are events that are beyond our control but end up leaving our plants in ruins. Natural disasters like cyclones flood and drought can cause problems to the plants.

The cyclone can cause strong turbulent wind which will destroy the plants far beyond measure. It disperses the soil and even roots out the plants. The floods also wash away the plants. Floods are equally disastrous to the plants as they fall plants, uproot them, and damage them.

Drought, on the other hand, dries up the whole land. It dries every water and moisture of the soil to the extent that the plants dry up easily and completely.

However, these natural disasters can also create the perfect conditions for the plant to thrive. With other native vegetation drying off, being washed away, or dispersed by the turbulent wind, weed plants get the avenue to enjoy all the nutrients in the land all to itself. To this effect, the plant gets little or no competition from the native vegetation.

4. **Fire:** It is important to note that the cannabis plant is highly flammable. One of the primary methods of taking in the cannabis plant is by smoking, thus be sure to keep fire far away from your farm. As a matter of fact, fire and weed hold a very complex relationship as it is very deadly and suppresses the rapid growth of the cannabis plant.

However, there is certain weed that often benefits from fire either directly or indirectly. Fire helps reduce the rate of competition by burning out other native plants in the farm. This would give the weed plant the necessary space it needs to thrive.

5. **Climate Change:** Climate change is not suitable for plants in general. But this is different in the case of marijuana. Cannabis' aggressive way of growing gives it an advantage over other native vegetation. It thrives

even in the harshest of conditions. Climate change impact is most severe on the plants.

Even though the Cannabis plant tends to grow in this condition, it won't reach its best in terms of yield and harvest. Climate change is often caused by variations, biotic processes, and human activities. In other words, it is also called global warming.

Some species or strains of weed that adapt to this severe climate condition end up with many advantages, which include more than enough space to expand their growth, little or no competition, and surplus nutrients.

Like the human body, even the cannabis plant needs nutrients to flourish. In a case where the soil lacks enough nutrients to nourish the plant, we would suggest you buy a fertilizer containing the necessary nutrients it needs to thrive. Additionally, no plant can survive in a severe environmental condition. Be that as it may, our next chapter will definitely be much more interesting. It promises to enlighten as well as familiarize you with the beautiful stage of the cannabis plant – Flower stage. Let's read through, shall we?

Chapter Thirteen
Outdoor Growing: Flowering and Breeding

Flowers are synonymous to most plants you would find out there. They blossom so brightly and beautifully, signaling the start of harvest. To this effect, when you see your cannabis plant sprouting flowers, then preparing for harvest is the next thing to do. However, before the cannabis plant reaches this far, it must have passed through lots of rigorous processes, techniques, and care.

The flowering stage of the cannabis life cycle is the most sensitive stage of the plant. This is when the plants need more than enough care and attention. Like we discussed in the previous chapters, the flowers are formed as a result of the male pollen sack being too ripe, thereby bursting all over.

This burst pollen sack disperses pollen all over the female plants. In turn, the female brings out white hair which would be visible at the internodes and top cola. In other words, these hairs are called "pistils". They start getting longer, thicker, and have more curl. They are mostly sticky and covered in resins.

According to expert growers, the cannabis plant produces these resins to capture pollen. Thus, if it fails to capture enough pollen, the plant (female) would produce more resins all over their body just to capture more of the male pollen when they are falling off.

The flowering period also will witness the plant filling out more than usual. The spaces between the branches and stems will be filled out appropriately, giving the cannabis plant a Christmas tree shape. There will be bigger leaves filling up each branch. The lower fan leaves will draw more of the sunlight. This will give the plant a better floral and leaf development.

To notice the peak of the flowering phase, the pistils of the female cannabis plant, which is located on the flower top, will swell. This swelling will make the pistil change color gradually. In most cases, it will change from white to brown. In other cases you will see it change from all white color to an orange tint, after which harvest is ready.

It is important to note that each strain or species of the cannabis plant comes with its own flowering moment and times. Each strain and species may also come with a whole different color when they reach their flowering peak.

Flushing the Cannabis Plant

We would advise you to always go through with this procedure whenever you are at the flowering stage or a few weeks before harvest. When you flush your plants, you basically put an end to the series of nutrients and fertilizers you feed them with. Only water that contains a neutral PH would be administered to the plants within these last few weeks.

How does flushing work? It's pretty simple. What flushing does is push out the salts and minerals in the soil. This will help give the plant a much better taste and scent, unlike the unpleasant, bad, and chemical-like taste and scent you could experience otherwise.

Also, during the flowering stage, you can choose to boost the quantity, quality, and caliber of the buds your plant's sprout. This is possible through the use of bloom fertilizers (as discussed in our previous chapter) and nutrients. Give the plants these blooming fertilizers during the first and second week of flowering.

This would make them grow taller and blossom more. The size of the plants you have in mind determines the extent of the fertilizers you should use. In a situation where you want your plant to be of small size with bigger buds, the bloom fertilizer is your best bet.

When the plant reaches the flowering stage, the production of THC increases drastically. This is very good for your plant if you intend to smoke it. The sticky nature of the THC gives the resin room for it to hold tight to the plant. THC is also used in permanent solutions to bug problems. It is also the flavor, the psychoactive substance, and the high that makes smoking cannabis intriguing.

Outdoor cannabis flowering stage is less stressful than with indoor growing. The outdoor nature gives the plant an edge as the earth tilts. Getting the necessary darkness for the flowering of the cannabis plant can be quite easy with the help of nature.

Breeding the Outdoor Cannabis

Breeding is a very important process of planting cannabis. Cannabis plants can be grown for two purposes which are:

1. As a means of reproduction
2. As an independent plant

Breeding is very easy when compared with other processes, techniques, and procedures that come with growing the cannabis plant. There are often strains that possess a great quality of plants and we would want to replicate them and those desired qualities. Breeding is the only way you can achieve those qualities.

If two plants of the same strain are bred, they end up producing seeds which contain almost all the same traits of the parent plants. It is important to note that the seeds might not contain all the traits of the parent plants. Both the offspring and parent will vary on either their level of potency, their color, the flavor in their taste and scent, etc.

This seed-making procedure is very easy. It is the process in which the male cannabis plant's pollen sac gets ripe and as a result, gets burst all over the female plants. This will pollinate the female plants and in the long run, the buds will hold seeds.

This pollen can be collected in cases where the male plant produces more than enough. They can be stored or preserved in film canisters for a period of 18 months. They can also be kept in freezers, pending the next harvest. When the male plant opens up their pods, it is best for you to carefully and gently collect this pollen. After getting enough, endeavor to shake off the remaining pollen on the female plants for pollination.

How to Breed Pure Strain

A lot of expert growers prefer replicating some seeds they bought with outstanding qualities instead of churning up strains to get a crossbreed or hybrid. To begin with, get the preferred seeds you would want to breed without mixing it up with other strains. It should be strictly similar strains. Afterward, sow the seeds and watch them grow. Be sure to allow your farm to contain just the strain you want. We would highly suggest you don't introduce or bring up new or foreign strains later.

Allow the male plants and the female plants to flourish well together. During the pollination phase, allow the male plant with the same strain as the female to pollinate. The end result will produce seeds of the same qualities. However, the qualities might not be a hundred percent replica of the parents.

How to Breed a Hybrid

Breeders are mostly fond of making new strains from the cannabis family. They often see planting and breeding of the cannabis plant as a way to showcase their love and passion for the hobby. This hobby has made them come up with a new form of weed, which is known to be called a hybrid. The hybrid is a crossbreed of two or more strains in producing an offspring with outstanding qualities. These qualities would be a mix of the parent qualities.

For instance, if a local dog mates with the foreign one, the offspring qualities would be the combination of both dogs. The offspring might pick the fine skin of the foreign dog, the long oral cavity of the local dog, the fine body build of the foreign dog, fluffy hair of the foreign dog, and so much more. This same thing applies to the cannabis plant.

The male plant from a different strain would be grown alongside a female plant of another strain. After pollination, you would notice that the seeds would be different. They would contain the mix qualities of both strains. However, they may also contain qualities the parent strains do not possess.

Thus, breeding may seem pretty easy, but trust me, it has its own fair share of complexity. If you are not knowledgeable about the procedure, your plant might start producing the wrong seeds. Be sure to familiarize yourself with the basics of genetics. Have an idea of how the genes work, which plant contains the homozygous, which is heterozygous, the phenotype of the plants, as well as the genotype.

These and more make up the important qualities and features of a strain. You can't just start crossbreeding plants of different strains without checking to see if they are compatible. A lot of beginners make this mistake, after which they would start searching the internet for answers to their problems.

Flowers and Breeding of the cannabis plant are two different things entirely. Where the former depicts the start of harvest, the latter entails the reproduction of similar strains or a whole new strain entirely. We are sure this chapter has helped you understand the importance and sensitivity of the flowering stage. Thus, we hope the next chapter would hold the same thrill. Let's turn the page over, shall we?

Chapters Fourteen
Harvesting the Marijuana Plants

Harvest is the end result of every plant. It is the long-lasting result all cannabis growers anticipate with much excitement. As a matter of fact, a certain thrill comes with the harvest. Knowing full-well that your plants of many weeks are to be harvested for the same purpose (cannabis intake) that motivated you in growing them can be quite intriguing.

Harvesting your cannabis plant marks the end of its life cycle. But before you start getting all excited, are you ready to face the stench smell it will produce during this stage? If no, then we would suggest you keep this in mind before proceeding to harvest your plants.

Most breeders attach a manual to their seeds. This manual also contains instructions to follow when harvest comes. Beginners often don't know when the plants have reached the harvest point. Sometimes, the flowering times which are written on the manuals are quite different from reality. The plant may present a whole different situation where the flowering times might come ahead or behind the breeder's timing.

The plants might start producing flowers a few weeks earlier than what was written in the manuals. To this effect, it is important to know when the plant reaches their harvest period through their features and appearance. Also, these changing features differ from each strain.

Indica Harvest

The Indica harvest is quite similar to the Sativa harvest. The Indica plant, which we discussed to be a 1-4 feet tall, should be cut down from the bottom, after which, you hang them in an upside-down posture. Remove as many of the fan leaves as you can. Do the same for the secondary leaves, but don't dump them in the same pile as the fan leaves. You can also clip out the trim of the plant. The trim makes up great quality weed. They are the leaves that have resins all over them.

Be that as it may, you now have more than two kinds of weed available at your disposal. Firstly, the fan leaves, which contain the lowest amount of THC. The secondary leaves, on the other hand, which possesses higher THC than the fan leaves. They are very intriguing and come with many flavors. Lastly, the trim, which happens to be the best leaves you can get in the Indica species. They are dipped in resins, which makes them much more potent than the other two leaves.

Sativa Harvest

Unlike the Indica harvest that doesn't require much work, the Sativa harvest is very strenuous and stressful as it contains lots of leaves and branches. The Sativa plant is over 10 feet tall. This is why outdoor growers like growing this plant more than its counterpart. Most times, they contain over 20 oz of buds. Now just imagine the heavy workload right in front of you!

First of all, we would advise you spread a sheet, or a canvas spread as the case may be, on the ground, so as to prevent the buds or leaves from falling to the ground. Just like the Indica plant, it must be cut down from the bottom and laid down on the canvas spread or sheet. Afterward, wrap them up nicely and gently with the canvas spread so they can be transported safely to where they would be harvested.

Just like the Indica plants, hang them upside down before carrying out the harvest process. Hanging them up without cutting off branches would present you with problems when clipping off the leaves as they would be too bushy and filled up.

Break off the branches and hang them up separately. After which you should proceed with clipping off the leaves as we have discussed in the Indica harvest section. Please note that too much direct light decreases the quantities of the THC. Where ever you plan on harvesting this plant must be relatively dark.

Harvest Time

Harvesting cannabis at the right time is vital. It would allow the bud to reach its maximum potential and growth, thereby making the THC much more potent. This is why many smokers end up rejecting some weed by merely looking at its appearance.

Additionally, choosing the right time to harvest your plants is influenced by a number of factors. According to expert growers, they believe harvest timing should be strictly a matter of personal preference. Sativa and Indica bloom phases differ. Thus, the harvest of the species varies in time. Here are some of the features to watch out for to tell the right timing;

Color Change

To begin with, there are a couple of ways to tell when it's time to harvest your cannabis buds. Perhaps the most reliable is to examine the color of the trichomes. These resin-bearing glands are considered the best standard of measurement as they are more consistent in their results than other recognition methods. In order to do this, you will need a magnifying glass—trichomes are quite tiny.

It is important to know that trichomes go through three consecutive color states. These are clear, cloudy, and amber. The best time to harvest is when half of the trichomes are amber, and half is clear or cloudy. This color disparity is due to the uppermost buds ripening earlier than the ones at the bottom. In any case, you don't want to wait for all trichomes to turn amber, as this generally leads to a decrease in THC.

Leaves Turn Yellow

This is one of the glaring features you would see in the plant. The yellow leaves are a good sign that your cannabis plant is ready to harvest. You can flush your plant when its large fan leaves start to turn yellow or when they fall off by themselves. But bear in mind that the falling of leaves is unlikely to happen when you use fertilizers.

Pistils

If you've got a photoperiod cannabis plant, then checking its pistils and stigmas is a useful way to gauge whether it's ready for the chop. You can usually assume that a plant is ready to harvest when about half of the pistils are brown. However, we would still recommend the trichome method as it is much more reliable.

Curling Leaves

This is one important clue to watch out for in the cannabis plant. The drying and curling of leaves is another sign that your cannabis plant is probably ready to be harvested. This happens because your cannabis takes less water as it nears its final phase of life. But be sure to confirm this method in conjunction with others, as there are pests and diseases that can cause dry and curling leaves.

Breeder Schedule

Like we said earlier, the breeder's timing might be wrong. But it's still a good way of timing your harvest. It is important to at least consider the harvest schedule provided by your seed source. This is usually found on the seed packaging. This schedule is the approximate number of days/weeks it will take for your cannabis seed to grow into a mature plant. This schedule, however, fluctuates based on growing conditions such as environment, water, and heat.

That is all you need to know to know about harvesting the Cannabis plant. What you do with your plant after that is totally up to you. Harvesting the plant comes with excitement and thrill. It is the final reward for the hard work you put in over the last couple of months. Feel free, enjoy your cannabis, it's the fruit of your labor. However, aside from smoking your harvest with friends, are there other things you might be able to use your cannabis plant for?

If you are interested in finding answers to that question, then we suggest you read on to the next chapter. You will surely be amazed at what you can do with your harvest.

Chapter Fifteen
After Harvesting, What's Next?!

I'm sure you must be thinking after harvesting your cannabis, smoking it with friends is the next thing to do. Well, you might be right, but you can't just start smoking wet leaves and buds. There are steps that need to be followed and procedures that need to be set in motion before smoking the plant can become a reality.

The process of growing cannabis does not stop at harvest time. Properly drying and curing your fresh cannabis stash is paramount to prevent mold contamination from taking place. These procedures will also result in buds that taste better and offer a superior high.

Drying and curing your Cannabis plant is a vital part of the final consumption process. It singles out your Cannabis plant from other organisms that may perch on the leaves, buds, and branches. When the leaves are clipped off during harvest, the leaves are left for a while. Please always remember not to mix the leaves up. The trimmed should be separated from the secondary leaves and the secondary leaves are separated from the fall leaves.

When setting out with the intention to grow cannabis, it's easy to see why harvesting handfuls of treasured buds is considered the pinnacle of the experience. All of the hard work, time, and money you've invested lead up to that final moment of reward. However, the work does not stop after the chop. It goes way beyond that.

The next thing growers do is to ensure that their harvest is processed correctly to prevent any chances of it becoming damaged or rendered non-smokeable. Drying and curing cannabis flowers post-harvest is an essential measure to minimize the risk of mold contamination. We wouldn't like to get our Cannabis plant spoilt at this final stage. Not when its consumption is just a few days away.

Drying and curing will also greatly improve the taste of a crop. This is due in part to processes that break down chlorophyll over time, resulting in a less-harsh taste. This aspect is especially important for those aiming to share their product or use it medicinally. Drying and curing are also reported to reduce the anxiety associated with smoking cannabis; it may even increase cannabinoid potency.

Trimming Before Drying

I'm sure a lot of people would have it at the back of their mind whether to let their plants dry before trimming or trim it while they are still wet. Nevertheless, the drying process begins as soon as you cut down your plants and begin to trim the buds. In doing so, you will notice how sticky and wet the fresh flowers are.

Although this stickiness is a good indicator of the sheer amount of psychoactive resin on your buds, it also offers a great breeding ground for fungal and bacterial contaminants. Leaving buds lying around in this state is usually a recipe for disaster; so it is best to act with haste.

There are multiple ways to trim your plants at the start of the drying process. "Wet trimming" involves trimming as soon as plants are ripe. Cut off the branches one by one and proceed to use sharp scissors or shears to precisely trim down excess plant matter. Although the buds are of primary interest, the sugar leaves also contain lower cannabinoid levels and can be stored separately, then made, for instance, into edibles later on.

"Dry trimming" is a technique mostly used when a grower has a large amount of plant matter and little time to process it. This involves cutting off branches and hanging them whole from drying lines. Once the plants are dry, they are then trimmed and processed. Dry trimming is more challenging when it comes to neatness as small sugar leaves will have curled in toward the bud. Plus, dry trimming may cause a loss of resin due to the agitation of the branches when hanging and being handled.

Regardless of the trimming method used, it is important to process your harvest within a suitable drying room. A drying room should ideally feature a cool and dark environment between 15-22°C.

The Drying Process

If you opt to use the wet trimming method, have your sticky buds at the ready. Now, you will need to spread them out across a large surface area. Placing them directly on cardboard or newspaper is not advised, as this does not subject the flowers to total aeration. Placing them upon a dry rack with netting or wire mesh is a far superior option. This allows airflow to reach all sides of the buds. If possible, use drying racks large enough to spread the buds out evenly, with a few centimeters between each one.

Using a small rack means piling buds on top of each other, which may result in uneven drying and possible mold contamination. When buds are left to dry, they start to release a lot of water. If this water cannot escape, pockets of moisture may begin to form. Moisture is one of the multiple variables that mold needs in order to proliferate.

Be that as it may, this chapter concludes the end of our amazing cannabis experience. You've successfully started the journey of growing your plant; you've taken the liberty of looking after the plant, nurturing them, and tending to them; a little patience in drying and curing them after harvest won't be a bad idea.

Conclusion

Wow, I'm sure you will agree with me that it has been a beautiful experience as you browsed through this handbook with rapt attention. We are also aware that before you picked up this book, you had been thinking growing cannabis is a big deal. Well, we hope we have cleared that perception. On the contrary, growing cannabis is fun!

It is exciting as well as rewarding. Now, before you start growing momentum and getting eager to start your cannabis farm, please ensure you check what the laws on cannabis are in your region. We wouldn't want to enter into this venture blindfolded.

Sow your seeds, tend to the plants, and harvest them when they are due, it's that easy. Even as a beginner or expert grower, we opened up your eyes to the possibilities around you when it comes to growing cannabis. But first thing first, remember the golden rule – Never tell anyone you are growing cannabis.

No one can be trusted. Even your best friend can rat you out. Keep the secret to yourself. There is a joy that comes with smoking your own cannabis as that is the end product of your labor. The flowering stage, like we discussed, is the most sensitive part of the plant's life cycle. Endeavor to give your plant the most needed attention during this stage.

Chapter by chapter, we discussed how to make your cannabis plant grow healthy and bear more buds. Some people might not entertain the idea of using a chemical like fertilizers to boost their plant. That is understandable, and there are other ways in which you can boost the rapid growth of your plant without resulting in the use of chemicals. Explore those ways we mentioned.

Notwithstanding, the issue of security is very vital in this kind of business. We are sure you must be getting used to that word as we used it in more than five instances in this handbook. Security is the bedrock of growing cannabis. If there is no security, your farm is highly vulnerable to everyone out there. Imagine a situation where everyone can go in and out of your cannabis farm with little or no security check. Not cool, right?

Focus on the brighter side. There is no business that doesn't come with risk. As a beginner, you might try growing cannabis more than once but end up getting frustrated with too many pests and small predator problem. Even before your plants reach flowering stage, these pests may have killed it off, making your effort looks useless.

Well, I've got news for you. Do not feel dissuaded. This handbook will help you through these obstacles.

Finally, you have all you need to grow a healthy-looking cannabis in one shot. Follow the steps, procedures, and processes we've discussed in the chapters of this book and the sky will not only be your limit but your starting point.

Good luck and God bless!

***

www.ingramcontent.com/pod-product-compliance
Lightning Source LLC
Chambersburg PA
CBHW071005080526
44587CB00015B/2350